Who is Man?

*The Raymond Fred West Memorial Lectures
at Stanford University
1963*

Who is Man?

Abraham J. Heschel

1965
Stanford University Press
Stanford, California

\

Stanford University Press
Stanford, California
© *1965 by Abraham J. Heschel*
Printed in the United States of America
L.C. 65-21491

To Hannah Susannah

I Chronicles 28:9–20

Preface

The following study comprises in expanded form the Raymond Fred West Memorial Lectures at Stanford University, delivered in May 1963.

Many important aspects of the problem of man have not been discussed in this volume, while others have been dealt with too briefly. But the volume will serve as prolegomena to a more comprehensive study in which I have been engaged for some time.

A. J. H.

Contents

Who is Man?

Chapter one

To think of man in human terms

To ask a question is an act of the intellect; to face a problem is a situation involving the whole person. A question is the result of thirst for knowledge; a problem reflects a state of perplexity, or even distress. A question calls for an answer, a problem calls for a solution (from the Latin *solvere,* to loosen, to dissolve).

No genuine problem comes into being out of sheer inquisitiveness. A problem is the outcome of a situation. It comes to pass in moments of being in straits, of intellectual embarrassment, in experiencing tension, conflict, contradiction.

To understand the meaning of the problem and to appreciate its urgency, we must keep alive in our reflection the situation of stress and strain in which it comes to pass, genesis and birth pangs, motivation, the face of perplexity, the varieties of experiencing it, the necessity of confronting and being preoccupied with it.

To clarify, to study, and to communicate a problem we must put it into words, for without translating the moments of wondering into logical terms there would be no possibility of testing the trans-subjective validity of what is thought in these moments, nor the possibility of its intersubjective communication.

Yet the act of verbalization extracts the problem from the situation in which it arises. The question verbalized, however, must not be equated with the problem confronting us. The danger always exists of those moments becoming distorted and even lost in the process of translation from situation to conceptualization. Too often speculation becomes analysis-by-long-distance of sounds transmitted over a poor connection. We formulate and debate the issues while oblivious to, and alienated from, the experiences or the insights which account for our raising the issues.

The predicament of much of contemporary philosophy is partly due to the fact that ongoing conceptualizations have so far outdistanced the situations which engender philosophizing that their conclusions seem to be unrelated to the original problems. After all, philosophy was made for man rather than man for philosophy.

A question is due to knowing too little, to a desire to know more; a problem is often due to knowing too much, to a conflict between opposing claims of knowledge. A question is the product of curiosity, a problem reflects an embarrassment of knowledge.

The impulse to reflect about the humanity of man comes from the conscience as well as from intellectual curiosity. It is motivated by anxiety, and not simply by a desire to add to the sum of information about a member of the class of mammals.

We are concerned with the problem of man because he is a being afflicted with contradictions and perplexities, because he is not completely a part of his environment. A good horse, properly cared for, lives as a part of his habitat and is unencumbered by problems. In sharp contrast, man is a problem intrinsically and under all circumstances. To be human is to be a problem, and the problem expresses itself in anguish, in the mental suffering of man. Every human being has at least a vague notion, image, or dream of what humanity ought to be, of how human nature ought to act. The problem of man is occasioned by our coming upon a conflict or contradiction between existence and expectation, between what man is and what is expected of him. It is in anguish that man becomes a problem to himself. What he has long disregarded suddenly erupts in painful awareness.

In our reflection we shall consider what man means to himself as well as what man means to his fellow man. The animality of man we can grasp with a fair degree of clarity. The perplexity begins when we attempt to make clear what is meant by the *humanity* of man.

What we aim at is not an analysis of a word as a semantic problem, but rather the investigation of a reality or a situation. Being human is not just a phrase referring to a concept within the mind, but a situation, a set of conditions, sensibilities, or prerequisites of man's special mode of being.

We can attain adequate understanding of man only if we think of man in human terms, *more humano,* and abstain from employing categories developed in the investigation of lower forms of life. The struggle for survival, for example, is not the same for human beings as it is for animals.

Sir Arthur Keith, a strong Darwinian, told his Aberdeen students in 1931: "Nature keeps her human orchard healthy by pruning. War is her pruning hook."* According to a Ger-

* New York *Times,* January 8, 1955, obituary page.

man general, "War is a biological necessity of the first importance, a regulative element in the life of mankind which cannot be dispensed with.... But it is not only a biological law but a moral obligation and, as such, an indispensable factor in civilization."* "God will see to it," says Treitschke, "that war always occurs as a drastic medicine for the human race."§

We are concerned with the totality of man's existence, not only or primarily with some of its aspects. Vast scientific efforts are devoted to the exploration of various aspects of human life—for example, anthropology, economics, linguistics, medicine, physiology, political science, psychology, sociology. Yet any specialized study of man treating each function and drive in isolation tends to look upon the totality of the person from the point of view of a particular function or drive. Such procedures have, indeed, resulted in an increasing atomization of our knowledge of man, in the fragmentation of the personality, in metonymical misunderstandings, in mistaking the part for the whole. Is it possible to comprehend one impulse separately, disregarding the interdependence of all impulses within the wholeness of the person?

Do we live what we are?

What is it that we seek to know? What does the knowledge of man aim at? What knowledge or object of knowledge do we question when we raise the question about him? What does the question about man hope to accomplish?

Man is not a *tabula rasa*. Unlike other objects, the desire to know himself is part of his being. To know himself he must

---

* Friedrich von Bernhardi, *Germany and the Next War* (New York, 1914), ch. 1.
§ *Ibid.,* p. 17.

first question himself, and that means questioning his self-knowing, disturbing what may be a narcissistic relationship of the self to its conceits, ingrown thinking. To raise such questions is more than to seek an approach to an answer; it is a breakthrough.

The task of a philosophy of man cannot be properly defined as a description of the nature of human being. It is critique as well as description, disclosure of possibilities as well as exposition of actualities of human being. The trend of our thinking leads us not only to form questions about human being but also to question human being. We question what we are in the light of an intuitive expectation or a vision of what man ought to be.

Something is meant by human being which involves more than just being; something is at stake in human being which is obscured, suppressed, disregarded, or distorted. How to penetrate the shell of his adjustments and to inquire whether adjustment is his ultimate vocation? We study human behavior; we must not disregard human bewilderment. We analyze expression; we must not disregard the inability to express what we sense. We know more about man's possessions than about his moods. We describe deeds; we must not fail to explore how one relates inwardly to what one does.

Do we live what we are or do we live what we have, or by what we have? Our difficulty is that we know so little about the humanity of man. We know what he makes, but we do not know what he is. In the characterizations of man, for example, as a tool-making or thinking animal, reference is made to the functions, not to the being, of man. Is it not conceivable that our entire civilization is built upon a misinterpretation of man? Or that the tragedy of modern man is due to the fact

5

that he is a being who forgot the question: Who is man? The failure to identify himself, to know what is authentic human existence, leads him to assume a false identity, to pretend to be what he is unable to be or to fail to accept what is at the very root of his being. Ignorance about man is not lack of knowledge but false knowledge.

Self-knowledge is part of our being

Man is not free to choose whether or not he wants to attain knowledge about himself. He necessarily and under all circumstances possesses a degree of such knowledge, preconceptions, and standards of self-interpretation. The paradox is that man is an obscure text to himself. He knows that something is meant by what he is, by what he does, but he remains perplexed when called upon to interpret his own being. It is not enough to read the syllables of a text written in a language which one does not understand, to observe and to recount man's external behavior, important and necessary as such an enterprise is. Man must also interpret them in terms larger than his inner life.

What is the right method of exegesis of human existence?

The philosopher's primary task is not merely to describe and to judge the modes and facts of man's actual behavior, but also to examine and to understand the meaning of describing and judging the modes and facts of his behavior. We obviously judge the behavior of man by standards which we do not apply to the hippopotamus. Is it not possible that our standards are unfair? Is it not conceivable that we expect too much or too little of man? Man was, is, and will always remain a beast, and nothing beastly is alien to him. And yet such an epigram, though rationally plausible, is intuitively repulsive. Is that re-

6

pulsiveness intrinsic to our existence as human being? Or is our acceptance of nonbeastly standards a stratagem designed to protect our beastly instincts?

In asking about man we ask of man what he knows about himself as a human being. This self-knowledge is part of his being. Thus, knowing oneself and being a self are not to be kept apart.

Like all concrete beings, man occupies a place in physical space. However, unlike other beings, his authentic existence goes on in an inner space. Geography determines his physical position; his thoughts are his personal position. The thought we think is where we are, partly or entirely. The thought we think is the space of the inner life, comprehending it. A person is in his thoughts, particularly in the way in which he knows or understands his own self. His thoughts are his situation. His nature includes what he thinks he is.

Unlike a theory of things which seeks merely to know its subject, a theory of man shapes and affects its subject. Statements about man magnetize the inner space of man. We not only describe the "nature" of man, we fashion it. We become what we think of ourselves.

We use the term "nature" in contrast to culture, natural in contrast to artificial, to denote that which has not been changed and affected by human action, free from calculations and conscious design, completely artless, abiding in the state in which it has come into being. In this sense the natural man is a myth and a contradiction in terms, because man has become man by acts of culture, by changing his natural state.

Human nature in its pristine, uncorrupted state is not given to us. Man as we encounter him is already stamped by an image, an artifact. Human being in distinction from all other

7

beings is endowed with consciousness of its own being, not only with awareness of the presence of other beings. Consciousness-of implies awareness of one's special position in relation to other beings. Any conception as to what I am going to do with myself presupposes my having an image of myself.

It is questionable whether man's nature can be treated as "a substance" in isolation. Behavior is determined not only by processes inside such a substance, but also by forces and standards that prevail in society, by heterogeneous pressures from the outside. What is given is a complexity. The decisions, norms, preferences affecting both action and motivation are not simply part of human nature; they are determined by the image of man we are committed to, by the ultimate context to which we seek to relate ourselves. Man is endowed with an amazing degree of receptivity, conformity, and gullibility. He is never finished, never immutable. Humanity is not something he comes upon in the recesses of the self. He always looks for a model or an example to follow. What determines one's being human is the image one adopts.

Thus the truth of a theory about man is either creative or irrelevant, but never merely descriptive. A theory about the stars never becomes a part of the being of the stars. A theory about man enters his consciousness, determines his self-understanding, and modifies his very existence. The image of man affects the nature of man. Any attempt to derive an image from human nature can only result in extracting an image originally injected in it.

The implications of being human

There is no substitute for the work done by the various sciences dealing with man. Yet there is an urgent need for an approach seeking to identify what is unique about the humanity of man, a task beyond the scope of the sciences mentioned above.

Behavioral sciences have enriched our knowledge of psychological, biological, and sociological facts and patterns of behavior by observation and description. However, we must not forget that in contrast to animals man is a being who not only behaves but also reflects about how he behaves. Sensitivity to one's own behavior, the ability to question it, to regard it as a problem rather than as a structure consisting exclusively of irreducible, immutable, and ultimate facts, is an essential quality of being human. The fact that to the mind of man his behavior is a problem instead of an unquestioned immutable fact is as important a datum of inner activity as the facts of external behavior.

Empirical intemperance, the desire to be exact, to attend to "hard" facts which are subject to measurement, may defeat its own end. It makes us blind to the fact behind the facts—that what makes a human being human is not just mechanical, biological, and psychological functioning, but the ability to make decisions constantly. Facts exhibited in life, cut off from antecedent decisions and determinations, from simultaneous attitudes as well as from subsequent reactions and reflections, cannot be exactly described.

It is an intellectually stifling assumption to regard a behavior pattern as a matter of fact pure and simple, just because it can submit itself to exact methods of inquiry. Is it not a fallacy to regard a behavior pattern as if it were a ghost city, an agglomeration of buildings with no living soul dwelling therein? A human behavior pattern is not a monument to a life that is gone, but a drama full of life. It is a system as well

9

as a groping, a wavering, a striking forth; solidity as well as outburst, deviation, inconsistency; not a final order but a process, conditioned, manipulated, questioned, challenged, and guided by a variety of factors.

The more refined and accessible the avenues to the study of behavioral facts become, the greater the scarcity of intellectual audacity in probing what is imponderable about human being.

Our understanding of man is dangerously incomplete if we dwell exclusively on the facts of human being and disregard what is at stake in human being. The facts, man's actual behavior, are explicit; what is at stake is implied. Since behavior patterns may be easily observed and described with a degree of statistical precision, we are inclined to reduce all of man to what is explicit, manifest, observable.

It is a mistake, however, to equate man's essence with his manifestations. The power and secret of his being reside as much in the unsaid and unproclaimed, in the tacit and ineffable, in the acts of awareness that defy expression as in the vessels man creates for his expression.

Physical things can be defined in terms of objective properties; man can be understood only in terms of his total situation, in terms of the demands he is called upon to answer. The chief problem of man is not his nature, but what he does with his nature.

Human being, therefore, must not be reduced to human nature. Human being is a fact as well as a desideratum, a given constellation as well as an opportunity. It can be understood only in relation to a challenge. It includes both the process and the structure of the facts of his being as well as the surprise and the events that come to pass in his existence.

The self as a problem

Our intention, therefore, is not to engage in a purely descriptive exploration of the total scope and pattern of human behavior, but to ascertain ends and directions, asking questions and raising issues which are implied in description. The task of our inquiry is to explore modes of being which characterize the uniqueness of being human. What constitutes human existence? What situations and sensibilities belong necessarily to the make-up of being human?

Man is never neutral or indifferent in relation to his own self. Love and knowledge, value judgment and factual description cannot be kept apart in establishing self-knowledge. Self-knowledge embodies either acceptance or rejection. One's relationship to the self is inconceivable without the possession of certain standards or preferences of value.

The notion of the strict contrast between descriptive and normative, analysis and evaluation, observation and interpretation, loses its relevance in the process of man seeking to establish his being human.

Facts of personal existence are not merely given. They are given through self-comprehension, and self-comprehension is an interpretation, since every act of self-comprehension involves the application of value judgments, norms, and decisions, and is the result of a selective attentiveness, reflecting a particular perspective. Thus even the facts of my existence are disclosed to me by way of interpretation, the terms of which determine the mode of my living and self-understanding.

Self-understanding can hardly be kept strictly within the limits of description of facts, since the self itself is a compound of facts and norms, of what *is* as well as of a consciousness of what *ought* to be. The essence of being human is value, value involved in human being.

As said above, the problem of man is occasioned by our coming upon a conflict or contradiction between existence and expectation. Thus the root of self-understanding is in the awareness of the self as a problem; it operates as critical reflection. Displacement of complacency, questioning the self, its acts and traits, is the primary motivation of self-understanding.

Self-understanding is entirely dependent upon self-judgment, and must not be equated with observation or self-observation. Mere description, simple dogmatic acceptance of the self, amounts to the deproblematizing of the man and is really the cessation of self-understanding. In short, if being human continues to be a problem, we must realize that the method of description, used exclusively, can at best offer us self-observation but is incapable of dealing with the problem.

Care for man

Wondering is a mode of human being. But wondering may just be sheer wandering, moving aimlessly, roaming, rambling. Channeling our wondering into the form of a question is the imposition of a pattern and a procedure upon the mind.

There is more than one question that can be asked. The choice of question determines the trend of the inquiry. In other words, each question is a preconceived pattern, and there is more than one pattern. A pattern orders the inchoate wondering and determines in advance the process of thinking about its theme.

To know that a question is an answer in disguise is a minimum of wisdom. This is the thought that comes to all men, to every man in the form of question: What am I here for? What is at stake in my existence? This question is not derived from premises. It is given with existence. Man, a problem to himself, does not take his existence for granted.

We must always start from the beginning. The most vital problems cannot be settled vicariously. No solution is established once and for all. We must all ponder the same question and wonder at the same puzzle. Just as I had to go through childhood, adolescence, and maturity, so must I go through the crises, embarrassments, heartaches, and wrestlings with this basic issue.

In asking the question about man, I have in mind not only a question about the essence but also a question about the concrete situation in which we find ourselves, a situation that puts the problem of man in a new light. The issue is old, yet the perspective is one of emergency. New in this age is an unparalleled awareness of the terrifying seriousness of the human situation. Questions we seriously ask today would have seemed utterly absurd twenty years ago, such as, for example: Are we the last generation? Is this the very last hour for Western civilization?

Philosophy cannot be the same after Auschwitz and Hiroshima. Certain assumptions about humanity have proved to be specious, have been smashed. What has long been regarded as commonplace has proved to be utopianism.

Philosophy, to be relevant, must offer us a wisdom to live by—relevant not only in the isolation of our study rooms but also in moments of facing staggering cruelty and the threat of disaster. The question of man must be pondered not only in the halls of learning but also in the presence of inmates in extermination camps, and in the sight of the mushroom of a nuclear explosion.

What is happening in the life of man, and how are we to grasp it? We ask in order to know how to live.

The nature of our inquiry stands in marked contrast to other inquiries. Other issues we explore out of curiosity; the issue of man we explore out of personal involvement. In other issues inquirer and theme are apart: I know the Rocky Mountains, but I am not the Rocky Mountains. Yet in regard to knowledge of myself I am what I seek to know; being and knowing, subject and object, are one. We have seen that we cannot reflect about the humanity of man and retain a relationship of complete detachment, since all understanding of man is derived from self-understanding, and one can never remain aloof from one's own self.

The most valuable insights into the human situation have been gained not through patient introspection or systematic scrutiny, but rather through surprise and shock of dramatic failures. Indeed, it is usually in the wake of frustration, in moments of crisis and self-disillusionment, and rarely out of astonishment at man's glorious achievements, that radical reflection comes to pass.

This is an age in which it is impossible to think about the human situation without shame, anguish, and disgust, in which it is impossible to experience enjoyment without grief and unending heartache, to observe personal triumphs without pangs of embarrassment.

Why do we ask the question about man? Because the knowledge about man which we had accepted as self-evident has proved to be a mass of bubbles bursting at the slightest increase in temperature. Some of us live in dismay caused by what man has revealed about himself.

The sickness of our age is the failure of conscience rather than the failure of nerve. Our conscience is not the same. Stultified by its own bankruptcy, staggered by the immense complexity of the challenge, it becomes subject to automation. Pride in our immediate past would be callousness, just as optimism about the immediate future would be stupidity. In the period of Enlightenment a major concern of philosophy was to emancipate man from the clutches of the past. Today our concern seems to be to protect ourselves against the abyss of the future.

One cannot study the condition of man without being touched by the plight of man. Though biologically intact, man is essentially afflicted with a sense of helplessness, discontent, inferiority, fear. Outwardly Homo sapiens may pretend to be satisfied and strong; inwardly he is poor, needy, vulnerable, always on the verge of misery, prone to suffer mentally and physically. Scratch his skin and you come upon bereavement, affliction, uncertainty, fear, and pain. Disparity between his appearance and reality is a condition of social integration. Suppressions are the price he pays for being accepted in society. Adjustment involves assenting to odd auspices, concessions of conscience, inevitable hypocrisies. It is, indeed, often "a life of quiet desperation."

The logic of being human

The aim is an inquiry into the logic of being human. What is meant by being human? What are the grounds on which to justify human being's claim to being human? Is the humanity of man an incontestable insight, a basic assumption of man, as intrinsic to human being as the ability to count or the capacity to walk on two legs? Or is it a whimsical dream, a changing, contingent, and accidental state of mind to be explained psychologically as derivative? In other words, does being human belong to human "nature" as a necessity of being or is it an epiphenomenon, a superimposed veneer easily rubbed off?

We stand surprised at what is disclosed in our experience of humanity. Being human is a reality. Man's being human is constituted by his essential sensibilities, by his modes of response to the realities he is aware of—to the being that *I* am, to the beings that surround *me,* to the being that transcends *me*—or, more specifically, by how he relates to the existence that he is, to the existence of his fellow men, to what is given in his immediate surroundings, to that which *is* but is not immediately given.

In his facticity man's notions of being human are both vague and confused; they are more frequently reflected in moods than in decisions. Are these notions, then, devoid of ontological validity? People continue to consume food long before they are aware of the necessity of nutrition. Yet it would be misleading to regard the consumption of food as a mere psychological need. The liquidation of being human would inevitably lead to the liquidation of human being. There is the ontological connective between human being and being human. Awareness, for example, of life's significance is not just a psychological need, it is part of man's being human.

Being human and human being are interdependent, and the components of the former are inherently related to the facts and the drives of the latter. What am I aware of when

I think of the existence that I am? What do I sense about my existence as being human?

Being human, I repeat, is inherent as a desideratum in human being. It is not given explicitly but is interpreted by experience.

Our inquiry must begin with an analysis of the content of this awareness. Is there a pattern to be found in man's understanding of this basic insight? What do we mean when we say "being human"? Do we face changing meanings of permanent insights or permanent meanings of changing insights? Can we agree at least in rejecting alternatives to certain meanings we cherish? Can we agree on a notion of what contradicts being human? We assume that the term "human" retains some sameness of meaning when used repeatedly on different occasions. Are there any permanent, necessary, or constitutive features of the desideratum? How shall we articulate exactly what is sensed by us vaguely?

Chapter two

Some definitions of man

Whom do I mean when I ask about man? I mean myself as well as other selves. The subject I ask about is exceedingly close to me. I not only perceive it; I am it as well as representing it. To know others I must know myself, just as understanding others is a necessary prerequisite for understanding myself.

The maxim "Know thyself" which was inscribed at the gate of the Temple of Apollo at Delphi referred to self-knowledge in relation to the gods: "Know that you are human and nothing more"—a warning against presumption (*hybris*), and a call to the Apollonic virtue of temperance (*sophrosyne*).* It was Socrates who isolated the nature of man as a problem in itself, regardless of his relation to the gods, and employed the maxim "Know thyself" in the sense of self-examination.§ Man must interrogate his own nature; through self-knowledge men

* See *Charmides* 164; Martin Nilsson, *Greek Piety* (Oxford, 1948), pp. 47f; also A. Altmann, "The Delphic Maxim in Medieval Islam and Judaism," in *Biblical and Other Studies,* ed. A. Altmann (Cambridge, Mass., 1963), pp. 183ff.

§ *Phaedrus* 230. It is also ascribed to Thales: Diogenes Laertius *Thales,* section 40.

18

meet with countless blessings, and through ignorance of themselves with many evils.*

Regarded by Plato as the very essence of knowledge, "Know thyself" was later characterized as a brief saying, and yet a task so great that Zeus himself alone could master it.§ There is no issue about which so many contradictory statements have been made, no issue so important, no issue so obscure. Psychology, biology, sociology have sought to explore the nature of man. And yet man remains an enigma.

This failure, standing in such marked contrast to the advancement of our knowledge about other matters, is itself a major problem. Why is man elusive in spite of his being the most self-expressive entity known to us?

The right knowledge of man is a prerequisite for the right understanding of man's knowledge about the world. All decisions, cognitive, moral, aesthetic, are determined by the conception of our own selves.

Protagoras maintained: "Man is the measure of all things."¶ This naturalist principle has been shattered more than ever in our own age by the question: What is the measure of man? Postmodern man is more deeply perplexed about the nature of man than were his ancestors.

In efforts to comprehend the nature of man, numerous definitions have been suggested which have enhanced our realistic understanding and illumined many aspects of man's nature

---

* Xenophon *Memorabilia* IV, 2, 24.

§ According to Menander, "the saying 'Know thyself' is not well said. It were more practical to say, 'Know other folks.'" See Menander, *The Principal Fragments,* ed. Frances G. Allinson (New York, 1930), p. 361 (Thrasyleon).

¶ Diogenes Laertius *Protagoras,* book 9, section 51.

and condition. And yet they fall short of helping us in our situation today when ultimate problems have become our immediate problems.

What is man? A worm crawling on a pebble, the earth; a speck of life floating aimlessly through the immeasurable vastness of the universe.

"In the final analysis, man's 'soul' is no more than his heat-producing metabolism and warm blood, lung respiration and breath, his inordinately large brain and questing mind, the creativity of his hands, his memory, dreams, and volition, his familial social organization, conscience, and culture."*

We know that man is more similar to an ape than an ape is to a toad. It may be that "man has not only developed from the realm of animals; he was, is, and shall always remain an animal." But is this the whole truth about man?

Indeed, man is a thing of space, biologically a type of mammal, and the definitions cited above expose aspects of the facticity of his being. However, when pretending to express what is decisive or central about man, these definitions seem to depict an effigy rather than an image of man. We are ready to accept as adequate the definition of a dog as a carnivorous domesticated mammal and of a fish as of the class of vertebrate animals living exclusively in water. But are we ready to accept the defintion of a human being as an individual of the highest type of mammal existing or known to have existed?

What do we seek to know?

These definitions betray a deep inclination to conceive man as a being made in the image of the animal. There undoubtedly is a conscious desire in man to be animal, "natural" in

* Weston La Barre, *The Human Animal* (Chicago, 1954), p. 295.

the experience of carnality, or even to identify himself as animal in destiny and essence. It is, however, questionable whether this desire may serve as a key in solving the riddle of human being. Is it to be regarded as evidence of man's being an animal at heart or as a desire to experience what he is not?

Since Aristotle it has been the generally accepted procedure to define man as a unit in the animal kingdom. Man was defined by Aristotle as "by nature a civilized animal," and "an animal capable of acquiring knowledge," as an animal that walks on two feet, as a political animal, as the only animal that has the power of choice, as the most imitative animal.* Scholastic philosophy accepted the definition of man as an *animal rationale,* and Benjamin Franklin defined him as Homo faber, a tool-making animal.

This tendency—so widespread in anthropological reflection —to comprehend man in comparison with the animal, from the perspective of what we know about the animal, is bound to yield answers which are unrelated to our question. To be sure, anatomy and physiology display innumerable points of resemblance between man and animal. Yet, for all the similarity in composition and functions, the contrasts are even more remarkable. In asking the question about man our problem is not the undeniable fact of his animality but the enigma of what he does, because and in spite of, with and apart from, his animality. The question about man is not provoked by what we have in common with the animal kingdom, nor is it a function derived from what is animal in man.

* *Topica* 128^b 17, 132^a 8; *Topica* 130^b 8, 132^a 20, 133^a 21, 134^a 15, 140^a 36; *Topica* 133^b 8, 136^b 20, 140^b 33; *Politika* 1253^a 1; *Ethica Eudemia* 1226^b 22; *Poetica* 1448^b 8.

In establishing a definition of man I am defining myself. Its first test must be its acceptability to myself. Do I recognize myself in any of these definitions? Am I ready to identify myself as an animal with a particular adjective?

In order to understand the validity of an answer, it is necessary, as said above, to comprehend the precise and full meaning of the problem, the situation of stress and strain in which it comes to pass, and the necessity of coming to grips with it. Otherwise, we are likely to accept answers that are irrelevant to the questions.

Man in search of self-understanding is not motivated by a desire to classify himself zoologically or to find his place within the animal kingdom. His search, his being puzzled at himself is above all an act of disassociation and disengagement from sheer being, animal or otherwise. The search for self-understanding is a search for authenticity of essence, a search for genuineness not to be found in anonymity, commonness, and unremitting connaturality. Thus any doctrine that describes man as an animal with a distinguishing attribute tends to obscure the problem which we seek to understand. Man is a peculiar being trying to understand his uniqueness. What he seeks to understand is not his animality but his humanity. He is not in search of his origin, he is in search of his destiny. The way man has come to be what he is illumines neither his immediate situation nor his ultimate destination. The gulf between the human and the nonhuman can be grasped only in human terms. Even the derivation of the human from the nonhuman is a human problem. Thus, pointing to the origin of man throws us back to the question: What do we mean by man, whose origin we try to explore?

The hippopotamus may well regard man, with his physical

weakness, emotional unpredictability, and mental confusion, as a freak, as an unhappy and perverse sort of animal. However, in asking about the status of man we obviously take the perspective and standards of man. What do these standards disclose about the inner being of man?

Is it not possible that, in following the example of Aristotle and contemplating man in terms of the animal species, we have been looking at man from the wrong perspective? The sense in which the term "animal" is used in defining the whole man is far from being clear and exact. Do we really know the inner life of the animals? Is it possible for us to sense pure animality, unmixed with humanity? Is the animality of a human being the same as the animality of an animal? Would it be valid to define an ape as a human being without the faculty of reason and the skill of making tools?

It is reported that after Plato had defined man to be a two-legged animal without feathers, Diogenes plucked a cock and brought it into the Academy. The zoomorphic conception of man enables us to assign his place in the physical universe, yet it fails to account for the infinite dissimilarity between man and the highest animal below him. Zoomorphic conceptions of man are as proper as anthropomorphic conceptions of God. In addition to its descriptive inadequacy, the suggestive and evocative meaning of the word "animal" in the term "thinking animal" distorts as much as it clarifies.

Every generation has a definition of man it deserves. But it seems to me that we of this generation have fared worse than we deserve. Accepting a definition is man's way of identifying himself, holding up a mirror in which to scan his own face. It is characteristic of the inner situation of contemporary man that the plausible way to identify himself is to see himself in the image of a machine. "The human machine" is today a more acceptable description of man than the human animal. Man is simply "a machine into which we put what we call food and produce what we call thought." A human being is "an ingenious assembly of portable plumbing." The definition itself goes back to the eighteenth century.[*] Never before, however, has it been so widely accepted as plausible. An animal stands before us as a mystery; a machine is an invention.

We must not take lightly man's pronouncements about himself. They surely reveal as well as affect his basic attitudes. Is it not right to say that we often treat man as if he were made in the likeness of a machine rather than in the likeness of God?

A definition of man in the Eleventh Edition of the *Encyclopaedia Britannica* is surely bound to inspire reverence for the greatness of man. It says: "Man is a seeker after the greatest degree of comfort for the least necessary expenditure of energy." Do we still recognize man here?

In pre-Nazi Germany the following statement of man was frequently quoted: "The human body contains a sufficient amount of fat to make seven cakes of soap, enough iron to make a medium-sized nail, a sufficient amount of phosphorus to equip two thousand match-heads, enough sulphur to rid one's self of one's fleas." Perhaps there was a connection between this statement and what the Nazis actually did in the extermination camps: make soap of human flesh.

---

[*] The first explicit statement *Man a Machine* goes back to *L'Homme machine*, the title of the famous work by La Mettrie (1709–51), in which human psychical activities are explained as mechanical functions of the brain. Descartes had denied the possibility of conceiving man as a machine (*Discourse on Method*, part V).

As descriptions of one of many aspects of the nature of man, these definitions may indeed be correct. But when pretending to express his essential meaning, they contribute to the gradual liquidation of man's self-understanding. And the liquidation of the self-understanding of man may lead to the self-extinction of man.

An important characteristic of our problem is that we do not even know how to phrase the question; we are bewildered and perplexed over what to ask about. What precisely do we wish to know in asking the question about man? Socrates articulates his desire to know himself as the desire to know man's disposition: "Am I a monster more complicated and more furious than the serpent Typhon, or a creature of a gentler and simpler sort, to whom Nature has given a divine and quiet lot?"*

However, what we seek to know about man is not only his disposition, the facts of life, but also his meaning and vocation, the goals of life. Beholding him piecemeal, we may come upon his kinship to animality. Seen as a whole, however, the situation of human being is one in which facts and goals, disposition and thirst for meaning are intertwined.

The eclipse of humanity

A new skepticism has emerged. In the past, philosophy has been motivated by a variety of ultimate questions. Can I be sure of what I know? Can I be sure of the reality of the external world? Today it is the humanity of man that is no longer self-evident, and the issue we face is: How can a human being achieve certainty of his humanity?

* *Phaedrus* 230.

In the Middle Ages thinkers were trying to discover proofs for the existence of God. Today we seem to look for proof for the existence of man.

The term "human" has become ambiguous. It has the connotation of weakness. ("He is only human." "Adam was but human." "To err is human." "All that I care to know is that a man is a human being—that is enough for me; he can't be any worse.") Yet the term is also used in the sense of magnanimity ("To step aside is human") as well as charity, particularly when spelled *humane,* which connotes feelings and inclination proper to man, having tenderness, compassion, and a disposition to treat other human beings and the lower animals with kindness. We speak of humane as opposed to severe or strict justice.

The ambiguity of Homo sapiens is an old triviality. Both praise and derision have been heaped profusely upon him. To some, he is "heaven's masterpiece"; to others, "Nature's sole mistake." Yet a note of compassion vibrates in the older discourses about him. Today we are fiercely articulate in deprecation and disdain. He who would write a book in the praise of man would be regarded as a half-wit or a liar. Man is being excessively denounced and condemned by artists, philosophers, and theologians. This is a typical view:

Since [Tennessee] Williams frankly declares himself to be an evangelist, we may inquire what is the gospel, the good news, which he has to offer. Man is a beast. The only difference between man and the other beasts is that man is a beast that knows he will die. The only honest man is the unabashed egotist. This honest man pours contempt upon the mendacity, the lies, the hypocrisy of others who will not acknowledge their egotism. The one irreducible value is life, which you must cling to as you can and use for the pursuit of pleasure and of power. The specific ends of life are sex and money. The great passions are lust and rapacity. So the human comedy is an outrageous medley of lechery, alcoholism, homosexuality, blasphemy, greed, brutality, hatred, obscenity. It is not a tragedy because it has not the dignity of a tragedy. The man who plays his role in it has on himself the marks of a total depravity. And as for the ultimate and irreducible value, life, that in the end is also a lie.*

Man has very few friends in the world, certainly very few in the contemporary literature about him. The Lord in heaven may prove to be his last friend on earth. Is it not possible that the tantrum we witness is due to our being trapped by overwhelming self-disdain, by a superior sense of inferiority?

The tragedy of this creeping self-disparagement is in its cultivation of the doubt whether man is worthy of being saved. Massive defamation of man may spell the doom of all of us. Moral annihilation leads to physical extermination. If man is contemptible, why be upset about the extinction of the human species? The eclipse of humanity, the inability to sense our spiritual relevance, to sense our being involved in the moral task is itself a dreadful punishment.

What is being human?

Man is our chief problem. His physical and mental reality is beyond dispute; his meaning, his spiritual relevance is a question that cries for an answer. Is it not right to suggest that the agony of the contemporary man is the agony of a spiritually stunted man? The image of man is larger than the frame into which he was contracted; we have underestimated

* Robert E. Fitch, "Secular Images of Man in Contemporary Literature," *Religious Education*, LIII, 87; also in *What Is the Nature of Man?* (Philadelphia, 1959), p. 60.

the nature of man. Even the form in which we ask the question about man is biased by our own conception of man as a thing. We ask: *What is man?* Yet the true question should be: *Who is man?** As a thing man is explicable; as a person he is both a mystery and a surprise. As a thing he is finite; as a person he is inexhaustible.

The popular definitions cited above offer an answer to the question "What is man?" in terms of his facticity, as a thing of space. The question "Who is man?" is a question of worth, a question of position and status within the order of beings.§

The self-certainty of the soul was valued by Augustine as the surest of all experiences. Now what is the soul certain of? It is certain that it thinks, that it functions. Yet the problem is not whether I function, or whether I am, but who I am.

And the first answer to the question: Who is man? is that he is a being who asks questions concerning himself. It is in asking such questions that man discovers that he is a person, and it is the kind of questions he asks that reveals his condition.

Our question is not only: What is the nature of the human species? but also: What is the situation of the human individ-

* "What is man?" means what sort of thing is he? "Who" is a pronoun asking for the identification of a person or persons. The biblical question: "What is man, that Thou art mindful of him..." (Psalm 8:4), "What is man, that Thou dost make so much of him..." (Job 7:17) really means what is the worth of man...?

§ The question "Who is man?" (phrased in the category of substance) is by no means the only possible question in a reflection about man. In an old rabbinic text three other questions are suggested: *"Whence* did you come?" *"Whither* are you going?" *"Before whom* are you destined to give account?" And yet these questions presuppose the knowledge of an answer to the question: "Who is man?"

28

ual? What is human about a human being? Specifically, our theme is not only: What is a *human being*? but also: What is *being human*?

Man is not only a special kind of being. His being human depends upon certain relations without which he ceases to be human. The decision to give priority to the question what is human about a human being is based upon the assumption that the category of human is not simply derived from the category of being. The attribute "human" in the term "human being" is not an accidental quality, added to the essence of his being. It is the essence. Human being demands being human. An analysis of the human situation discloses a number of essential modes of being human, a few of which I should like to refer to in the next chapter.

It is indeed conceivable that man may continue to be without being human. Human being and being human are both exposed to danger, the latter even more than the former. "Being human" must always be rescued from chaos or extinction.

One of the most frightening prospects we must face is that this earth may be populated by a race of beings which though belonging to the race of Homo sapiens according to biology will be devoid of the qualities by which man is spiritually distinguished from the rest of organic creatures. To be human we must know what being human means, how to acquire, how to preserve it.

Just as death is the liquidation of being, dehumanization is the liquidation of being human. What qualifies a being to be called a human being?

No one definition can fathom the depth of human being, the intricate ways and byways in whom it is disclosed. Yet to claim that the question is unanswerable, and the problem in-

29

soluble, would be to surrender to the hope of attaining any knowledge concerning significant issues, since the question about man is a radical question and the significance of all other questions we ask depends upon the answer we are ready to offer to this one.

Self-understanding seeks to comprehend my existence. What do I supremely care for? What do I dream of, aspire to? Facing myself as I am here and now I discover gold as well as dross. What I come upon as I delve within myself is twilight, confusion, contentment as well as not knowing what is ultimately worth striving for. The mind unguided is groping in the dark, the mind guided is the product of superimpositions.

Is it possible to achieve knowledge of the self? Rationalism operates with the assumption that whatever *is* can also be *known*. It fails to distinguish between the world as given *in* my mind, wrapped up in concepts and categories, and the world as given *to* my mind as sheer being; between the self as given *in* my explanations of certain behavioral forms and the self as given *to* my mind. What is the self? What in me remains identical throughout the changes and transformations to which I am subject, the forms of behavior, actions and reactions?

The minimum of self-awareness comes to expression in the words: I am. But who is I? And what does it mean to be?

The I is an epistemological pretext, a pseudonym for what we do not know. "I am" is a marvel, a source of astonishment. One can never recover from the surprise of just being here and now.

It seems that the depth and mystery of a human being is something that no analysis can grasp. The knowledge of man we get from science, for all its usefulness, strikes us as an oversimplification; its definitions prove barren when applied to actual human beings.

Ultimate self-penetration is neither possible nor desirable. What we may aim at is a degree of self-understanding which would enable us to project our living rather than let our living be a projection of crowd, a fashion or a whim. Our task must include the effort to discern and to disclose the authentic as well as the unauthentic prepossessions, the honest as well as dishonest manifestations of the inner life.

The exclamation of the Psalmist, "I am fearfully and wonderfully made!" (139:14) expresses man's sense of wonder at the mystery of his own existence. There is a depth of personal existence that cannot be fully illumined, that eludes our generalizations. Yet the necessity to understand man is rough and demanding.

To ex-plain means to make plain. Yet the roots of existence are never plain, never flat; existence is anchored in *depth*. One cannot study the life of a tree by *excavating its roots*.

What follows is an attempt to describe some modes of being human which every reader as a human being will recognize and accept as essential. They represent a requiredness rather than a fabrication of the mind; not postulates of morality but fundamentals of human existence. Failure in nurturing the essential sensibilities results in the decay of the humanity of the individual man.

These features or sensibilities are no disparate trifles, random impressions, arbitrarily registered, but rather necessary components which constitute the essence of being human. They are not reflecting actual behavior but rather the wisdom of a necessary self-awareness, a scope of interrelated features within which man must be understood in his being human

31

as distinguished from being animal, from being beastly. They are not simply given in man's consciousness, nor are they properties derived from his biological nature. His sheer being does not guarantee them. However, they may be claimed of him, expected of him. They emerge as manifestly true when a person begins to ponder the latent substance of his self-understanding.

Chapter three

Preciousness

What do I see when I see a man? I see him first as one other specimen of the human species, then as a specific, particular individual who can be named or identified; but then he stands before me as the only entity in nature with which sanctity is associated. All other sacred objects in space are made holy by man. Human life is the only type of being we consider intrinsically sacred, the only type of being we regard as supremely valuable. The particular individual may not be dear to me—in fact I may even dislike him. But he is dear to someone else, to his mother, for example, although that too is not the reason for his eminence. For even if nobody cares for him, he still is a human being.

Our way of seeing a person is different from our way of seeing a thing. A thing we perceive, a person we meet. To meet means not only to come upon, to come within the perception of, but also to come into the presence of, or association with, a person. To meet means not only to confront but also to agree, to join, to concur.

How do I think when I think of a human being? To think of a thing is to think what I know; to think of a human being is to think what I am. A thing I perceive in the light of my knowledge; a human being I see in the image of my own being. In perceiving an animal, I come upon otherness; in meeting a person, I come upon familiarity; "like knowing like." There is agreement of being, concurring of existence, a self beholding a self. I see what I am.

There are two ways of facing and inspecting human being: from within or from without. From within I face my own being, here-and-now; from without I encounter my fellow man's being-there. I suggest that although it is possible and legitimate to ponder being in general or the being of all beings, it is futile and impossible to ponder human being in general, the being of the human species, since my understanding of, and my relation to, my own being always intrudes into any reflection about the being of the human species. There is only one way of comprehending man's being-there, and that is by way of inspecting my own being.

What does my own being mean to me? What confronts me when I ponder my being here-and-now? My own being can never be comprehended as a sample of pure ontology. It can never be thought of as a pure fact.

My being here-and-now is not indifferent to me as another being there-and-now may be. Looking upon myself from the perspective of society or thinking comparatively, I am an average person. Facing myself intimately, immediately, I regard myself as unique, as exceedingly precious, not to be exchanged for anything else. I would not like my existence to be a total waste, an utter absurdity. No one will live my life for me, no one will think my thoughts for me or dream my dreams. My own being, placed as it is in the midst of many beings, is not simply being here too, being around, being part of the environment. It is at the very center of my consciousness that I am distinct.

It is through the awareness that I am not only an everybody that I evolve as a self, as somebody, as a person, as something that cannot be repeated, something for which there is no duplicate, no substitute. It is in the awareness of my being somebody that freedom comes to pass.

I am exceedingly noteworthy, exceedingly relevant to myself, and it is the notability of my existence that becomes elusive when looked upon from without, from the perspective of society, from the viewpoint of generalization. In other words, although my singularity is a matter of personal certainty to me, it looks like a conceit from the perspective of statistics or manpower administration. Luminous from within, my notability seems opaque if not absurd from without.

In the eyes of the world, I repeat, I am an average man. But to my heart I am not an average man. To my heart I am of great moment. The challenge I face is how to actualize, how to concretize the quiet eminence of my being.

Beyond all agony and anxiety lies the most important ingredient of self-reflection: the preciousness of my own existence. To my own heart my existence is unique, unprecedented, priceless, exceedingly precious, and I resist the thought of gambling away its meaning.

In the actual lives of actual men, life even when felt to be a burden is cherished deeply, valued supremely, accepted in its reality. The truth of human being is the love of being alive. It is as a result of extreme abuse and desecration of being that man brings upon himself the punishment of disgust with being.

Disgust of being, a sense of being trapped in the world, is

35

really a situation of being trapped in presumption. When man becomes his own idol, the tablets are broken. Is not the exaggerated anxiety about death due to presumption: the unspoken claim to go on living without dying?

"Man is obliged to say: It is for my sake that the world was created" (Sanhedrin 37a). There is a task that only I, and I alone, can carry out, a task so great that its fulfillment may epitomize the meaning of all humanity.

The fundamental problem of ethics has been expressed as the question: What ought I do? The weakness of this formulation is in separating doing from the sheer being of the "I," as if the ethical problem were a special and added aspect of a person's existence. However, the moral issue is deeper and more intimately related to the self than doing. The very question: What ought I to do? is a moral act. It is not a problem added to the self; it is the self as a problem.

The moral problem can be treated only as a personal problem: How should I live the life that I am? My life is the task, the problem, and the challenge.

The moral deed is important not only because the community, for example, needs it. It is important because without it there is no grasp of what is human about my being human. This formulation stands in contrast with another starting point for the moral inquiry: There are moral ideals and values; how shall I attain them?

Uniqueness

Why are we puzzled about man? Biologically man is easily defined or classified. Yet even though we may be able to define the human species and to place it in relation to the animal world, we quickly discover that such a definition is of little value in trying to understand the relations of man to man, or in our effort to understand our own selves.

It is the uniqueness of man that puzzles our mind. All other beings seem to fit perfectly into a natural order and are determined by permanent principles. Man alone occupies a unique status. As a natural being he is determined by natural laws. As a human being he must frequently choose; confined in his existence, he is unrestrained in his will. His acts do not emanate from him like rays of energy from matter. Placed in the parting of the ways, he must time and again decide which direction to take. The course of his life is, accordingly, unpredictable; no person can write his autobiography in advance.

Generalization, by means of which theories evolve, fails in trying to understand man. For in dealing with a particular man, I do not come upon a generality but upon an individuality, a person. It is precisely the exclusive application of generalities to human situations that accounts for many of our failures.

To my mind my existence is a course of events, a lifelong situation which is unique, a going-on-ness that cannot be repeated, for which there can be no substitute. My existence as an event is an original, not a copy. No two human beings are alike. A major mode of being human is uniqueness. Every human being has something to say, to think, or to do which is unprecedented. It is the crust, the make-up, the conformity, that tends to reduce existence to a generality.

Being human is a novelty—not a mere repetition or extension of the past, but an anticipation of things to come. Being human is a surprise, not a foregone conclusion. A person has a capacity to create events. Every person is a disclosure, an example of exclusiveness.

A human being has not only a body but also a face. A face cannot be grafted or interchanged. A face is a message, a face speaks, often unbeknown to the person. Is not the human face a living mixture of mystery and meaning? We are all able to see it, and are all unable to describe it. Is it not a strange marvel that among so many hundreds of millions of faces, no two faces are alike? And that no face remains quite the same for more than one instant? The most exposed part of the body, the best known, it is the least describable, a synonym for an incarnation of uniqueness. Can we look at a face as if it were a commonplace?

Individual examples of any kind of being are nameless; but every individual human being claims a name. A human individual is not a mere example or specimen of his species. You distort him by disregarding his uniqueness.

Being means striving to go on, to go along, to extend, to continue. Yet being human means to go beyond sheer continuity. Being human occurs, comes about in moments. Being human consists of outbursts of singularity. Singularity is a dimension easily forgotten, always threatened by the continuous assaults of wholesaleness. Sheer continuity leads to the suspension of singularity, drudgery, inner devastation, demolition of all moments. To discover the hospitality of being, one must cultivate the art of reaching beyond oneself. A life rising in outbursts into meaning is a way of sensing the beneficence of time.

No man is an average man. The ordinary, typical man, the common run undistinguished either by his superiority or by his inferiority, is the homunculus of statistics. In real life there is no ordinary, undistinguished man, unless man resigns himself to be drowned in indifference and commonness. Spiritual suicide is within everybody's reach.

Opportunity

The passage of being—of man or animal—is marked and fixed: from birth to death. The passage of being human leads through a maze: the dark and intricate maze we call the inner life of man. That maze must not be conceived as a structure, as a permanent setup; it is an exuberance that goes on, frequently defying pattern, rule, and form. The inner life is a state of constantly increasing, indefinitely spreading complexity. Left to himself, man of necessity goes astray; he is in need of guidance at every step.

Is there a guide for the labyrinth of man? The necessity of guidance is a mode of being human. Animal life is a straight path; the inner life is a maze, and no one can find his way through or about without guidance. Such is the condition from which there is no escape.

One thing that sets man apart from animals is a boundless, unpredictable capacity for the development of an inner universe. There is more potentiality in his soul than in any other being known to us. Look at the infant and try to imagine the multitude of events it is going to engender. One child named Johann Sebastian Bach was charged with power enough to hold generations of men in his spell. But is there any potentiality to acclaim or any surprise to expect in a calf or a colt? Indeed, the enigma of human being is not in what he is but in what he is able to be.*

* From A. J. Heschel, *Man Is Not Alone* (New York, 1951), p. 209.

39

What is obvious about man is a minimum of what is latent in him. It may be feasible to describe what the human species is; it is beyond our power to conceive what the human species is able to be.

Since the outstanding mark of man is the superiority of the possibilities of his being over the actuality of his being, we must not confine our understanding to what he is in his facticity. We must look beyond the facts in order to do justice to him. Man must be understood as a complex of opportunities as well as a bundle of facts.

To understand the problem of man in human terms we must not conceive of him in terms of physics, as a thing in which energy is stored away in some latent manner, but rather in categories of personal thinking and personal experience as a person who is called upon to be more than what he is. The task is not actualization of potentiality but understanding, acknowledging, answering, going beyond the status quo.

Nonfinality

Where is man? At what stage of his life and in what situation of his existence do we meet him as he really is? He is variable, fickle, appearing in different roles. Is he the same as father or mother as he is as salesman or soldier? Does he remain the same from the cradle to the grave, from the cave to the rocket?

All the definitions cited above have a ring of finality and presume to be definitive. However, there is no such entity as man in his permanent and final form. Man is rarely to be found in a definitive edition. A salient characteristic of being human is inconstancy both in behavior and in self-understanding, inability to remain what he is once and for all. Finality and humanity seem to be mutually exclusive. Man is caught in the polarity of being both tentative, undecided, unsettled as well as final, fixed, determined.

Anything is possible. The ambiguity of his traits and the ambivalence of his actions are such that his consistency involves inner contradiction. Man has many faces. Which is canonical and which is apocryphal?

To understand his being it is not enough to see him as he acts here and now, for example, as conditioned by our industrial society. Man is a being in flux. Yielding to a particular pattern of living he remains both compliant and restive, conforming and rebellious, captive and insurgent.

Animal being is thoroughly explicit, whereas human being is profoundly implicit. A stone is characterized by its finality, whereas man's outstanding quality is in his being a surprise.

To claim to be what I am not is a pretension. To insist that I must be only what I am now is a restriction which human nature must abhor. The being of a person is never completed, final. The status of a person is a *status nascendi*. The choice is made moment by moment. There is no standing still.

An elemental consciousness, free of all content, pristine and pure, has probably never existed. We certainly cannot conceive of pure consciousness, devoid of content, devoid of designs, intentions, implications, and conceptions. Thus we can only analyze the consciousness as it is already pregnant and filled with components.

It is a fatal illusion to assume that to be human is a fact given with human being rather than a goal and an achievement.

To animals the world is what it is; to man this is a world in the making, and being human means being on the way, striving, waiting, hoping.

Neither authenticity of existence nor the qualities of being human are safe properties. They are to be achieved, cultivated, and protected. We often live pretentiously, deceiving ourselves as well as others. Society, tradition, and conscience are all involved in us. To be human we must know what humanity means and how to acquire it. Our being human is always on trial, full of risk, precarious. Being human is an opportunity as well as a fact.

Process and events

In the awareness of my personhood I do not come upon sheer consciousness or a block of reality called the self, but upon the power to create events. Being human is not a thing, a substance; it is a moment that happens; not a process but a sequence of acts or events. The self that I am, the self that I come upon, has the ability to combine a variety of functions and intentions in order to bring about a result, the meaning or value of which transcends my own existence.

To be human is to intend, to decide, to challenge, not merely to go on, to react, or to be an effect. What is unique about man is in the way he relates himself to what is not in him. His existence is not a thing replete with energy but an interplay of a process and events.

What is the difference between process and event? A process happens regularly, following a relatively permanent pattern; an event is extraordinary, irregular. A process may be continuous, steady, uniform; events happen suddenly, intermittently, occasionally. Processes are typical; events are unique. A process follows a law, events create a precedent.

A process occurs in the physical order. But not all events

are reducible to physical terms. The life of Beethoven left music behind; yet valued in physical terms its effects on the world were felt less than the effect of a normal rainstorm or an earthquake.

Man lives in an order of events, not only in an order of processes. It is a spiritual order. Moments of insight, moments of decision, moments of prayer—these may be insignificant in the world of space, yet they put life into focus.

Nature is made up of processes—organic life, for example, may be described as consisting of the processes of birth, growth, maturity, and decay; history consists primarily of events. What lends human, historical character to the life of Pericles or Aristotle are not the organic processes through which they went but the extraordinary, surprising, and unpredictable acts, achievements, or events which distinguished them from other human beings.

An event is a happening that cannot be reduced to a part of a process. It is something we can neither predict nor fully explain. To speak of events is to imply that there are happenings in the world that are beyond the reach of our generalizations.

Being human is not a solid structure or a string of predictable facts, but an incalculable series of moments and acts.* As a process man may be described biologically; as an event he can only be understood creatively, dramatically. As a process life operates regularly. Its normality is in its repetitiousness; breakfast every morning, digestion every evening. However, everydayness, sameness, drearihood is a condition that stulti-

* A. J. Heschel, *God in Search of Man* (New York, 1955), pp. 209–10.

fies man's inner drives, affects negatively the process, the norm of which is repetitiousness. An extra ingredient which the positivist is unable to define goes into the make-up of human existence: the power to create an event. Deficiency of such power is a deadly sickness.

The alphabet of living is capable of forming a nearly infinite number of combinations, or situations. Yet some people have never acquired more than the spelling of one word: ditto, reducing all singularity to commonness.

The art of spelling the language of living involves man's relating himself to what is not in him, facing up to the truth that he is not simply around, that even boredom can be a creative clash. All terms of living tend to become stale. Inner renewal is a vital necessity.

Life lived as an event is a drama. Life reduced to a process becomes vegetation. The awareness of life as a drama comes about as a result of knowing that one has a part to play, of realizing that the self is unprecedented and of refusing to regard existence as a waste.

Solitude and solidarity

Self-sufficiency, independence, the capacity to stand apart, to differ, to resist, and to defy—all are modes of being human. There is no dignity without the ability to stand alone. One must withdraw and be still in order to hear. Solitude is a necessary protest to the incursions and the false alarms of society's hysteria, a period of cure and recovery.

The truth, however, is that man is never alone. It is together with all my contemporaries that I live, suffer, and rejoice, even while living in seclusion. Genuine solitude is not discarding but distilling humanity. Genuine solitude is a search for genuine solidarity. Man alone is a conceit. He is for the sake of, by the strength of, unknowingly and even knowingly involved in the community of man.

Man in his being is derived from, attended by, and directed to the being of community. For man *to be* means *to be with* other human beings. His existence *is* coexistence. He can never attain fulfillment, or sense meaning, unless it is shared, unless it pertains to other human beings.

Although it is true that in order to grasp the meaning of being human we analyze the human individual rather than the human species, any analysis that disregards social involvement, man's interdependence and correlativity, will miss the heart of being human.

Human solidarity is not the product of being human; being human is the product of human solidarity. Indeed, even the most personal concern, the search for meaning, is utterly meaningless as a pursuit of personal salvation. Its integrity discloses compassion, a hope or intuition of meaning in which all men may share.

Even preoccupation with the self, self-defense and self-aggrandizement, typical of all men, includes in its consciousness acknowledgment of the existence and dignity of other men. The prestige a person seeks involves respect for others whose recognition is desired. All achievements are born in the conviction that what is good for me will prove to be good for others.

"To be" is an intransitive verb; to be human, I repeat, is more than just to be. Man reflects about his being, and his reflection discloses to him that in order to be he must continually accept what is not his own, since being is never self-sufficient.

Reciprocity

Science is a way of interpreting experiences. For the self-understanding of man it is important to realize that experiences interpret and elucidate man.

The primary experience with which we begin in our infancy and continue in our childhood is *obtaining and seizing* things we care for. Developing and entering maturity we become involved in *giving and providing* for those we care for.

These are fundamental facts and must be recognized as primary data in the make-up of living, independent of motivations that may affect their intensity.

We receive continually; our very being is a gift in the form of an enigma; a breath of fresh air is inhalation of grace. Fullness of existence, personal being is achieved by what we offer in return. "How shall I ever repay to the Lord all the bounty He has given to me!" (Psalm 116:12) is a genuine question of man. *The dignity of human existence is in the power of reciprocity.*

For every new insight we must pay a new deed. We must strive to maintain a balance of power and mercy, of truth and generosity. Knowledge is a debt, not a private property. To be a person is to reciprocate, to offer in return for what one receives. Reciprocity involves appreciation. Biologically we all take in and give off. I become a person by knowing the meaning of receiving and giving. I become a person when I begin to reciprocate.

The degree to which one is sensitive to other people's suffering, to other men's humanity, is the index of one's own humanity. It is the root not only for social living but also of the study of humanities. The vital presupposition of the philosopher's question about man is his care for man.

The opposite of humanity is brutality, the failure to acknowledge the humanity of one's fellow man, the failure to be sensitive to his needs, to his situation. Brutality is often due to a failure of imagination as well as to the tendency to treat a person as a generality, to regard a person as an average man.

Man achieves fullness of being in fellowship, in care for others. He expands his existence by "bearing his fellow-man's burden." As we have said, animals are concerned for their own needs; the degree of our being human stands in direct proportion to the degree in which we care for others.

The central problem in terms of biblical thinking is not: "What is 'to be'?" but rather: "How to be and how not to be?"

The issue we face is not the dichotomy of being and misbeing, but that of righteous and unrighteous being. The tension is not between existence and essence but between existence and performance. For animals as well as for human beings when in peril and anguish the problem is to be or not to be. What distinguishes a human being is that his problem is *how* to be and *how* not to be. Indeed, man alone is motivated by the awareness of the insufficiency of sheer being, of sheer living. Man alone is open to the problem of how to be and how not to be on all levels of his existence.

Our first theme, then, is not what man is but how he is, not human being but being human, which is the sum of many relationships in which a human being is involved.

In the actual human situation "to be" is inseparable from "how to be." Thus on the level of his being human the process of his being stands over against him as a question: How should I live the existence that I am? Thus we see that the implied intent of the question, *Who is man?* is really, *How is man?*

Sanctity

As said above, man is the only entity in nature with which sanctity is associated. Sanctity of human life is not something we know conceptually, established on the basis of premises; it is an underived insight. It is not a quality that man can bestow upon himself; it is either bestowed upon us or spurious. We come upon it first in pondering the mystery of another person's life, and subsequently in the realization that one's own life is not something acquired or owned. Life is something *I am*. What I have is mine; what I am is not mine. Life is not my property.

Being human involves being sensitive to the sacred. The objects regarded as sacred may differ from country to country, yet sensitivity to the sacred is universal.

The acceptance of the sacred is an existential paradox: it is saying "yes" to a no; it is the antithesis of the will to power; it may contradict interests and stand in the way of satisfying inner drives.

To our sense of power the world is at our disposal, to be exploited to our advantage. To accept the sacred is an acknowledgment that certain things are not available to us, are not at our disposal. However, it is a profound misunderstanding to think of the sacred in terms of negativity. Its negativity and separateness is but a protective screen for the positive aspect of the sacred. For accepting the sacred means not only giving up claims, but also facing a unique dimension of reality.

What is the positive aspect of the sacred? Being a unique

quality, it is not capable of being described in terms of any other quality, just as beauty cannot be described in terms of goodness. The sacred is perceptible to the sense of the sacred. The beauty of a beautiful object is inherent in the object, whereas the sanctity of a sacred object transcends the object. Beauty is given with the nature of a thing, sanctity is imposed on things. Beauty is in the form of an object, sanctity in its status.

There are degrees of sanctity, but they all share one aspect: ultimate preciousness. To sense the sacred is to sense what is dear to God. Its mode of being differs from the modes of being of other qualities.

It is true that sacred objects are objects set apart from the rest of reality, but it is a mistake to regard the sacred and the profane as absolute contrasts. For some parts of reality to be endowed with sanctity, all of reality must be a reflection of sanctity. Reality embraces the actually sacred and the potentially sacred.

Chapter four

The dimension of meaning

We have expressed the problem of man in the form of asking: What is being human? Two other themes implied in our problem must be considered now.

1. What is being?
2. What is the meaning of human being?

The first theme dawns upon us in moments of radical amazement, when all answers, words, categories are suddenly disclosed to be a veneer, and the mystery of being strikes us as a problem that lurks behind many other problems. The second theme is not a question of semantics—how to define in reasonable terms the phrase "human being"—but one that goes far beyond the limits of self-understanding. It is an effort to understand the self (as well as all humanity) in terms larger than the self.

Human being is never sheer being; it is always involved in

Some paragraphs in this chapter are taken from my book *Man Is Not Alone* (New York, 1951), pp. 91ff., and from my study "The Concept of Man in Jewish Thought," in *The Concept of Man,* ed. S. Radhakrishnan and P. T. Raju (London, 1960), pp. 108–57.

meaning. The dimension of meaning is as indigenous to his being human as the dimension of space is to stars and stones. Just as man occupies a position in space, so has he a status in what may be called metaphorically a dimension of meaning. He is involved even when unaware of it. He may be creative or destructive; he cannot live outside it. Human being is either coming into meaning or betraying it. The concern for meaning, the gist of all creative efforts, is not self-imposed; it is a necessity of his being.

To the mind exposed to the reality that confronts us the paramount problem is being, yet to the mind attuned to the intimate human situation the excruciating, heart-rending problem is meaning. It is upon the intuition or affirmation of meaning that the sense of significant being—the sign of mental health—depends.

We would miss the aim of this search by reducing it to a search for the true self, for true being, for "human nature." The search is for significant being, for self-understanding as well as for belonging and attachment to a transcendent order of meaning. It includes an examination of the qualities of living that constitute significant being.

The attempt to identify the meaning of being a person or a human being is the indispensable prerequisite for bringing order into existence. It would be unfortunate for a person to live without a conventional name; it is disastrous for a person to live without inner identity. A name we simply receive and remember; spiritual identity we must strive for, come upon, acquire, enhance, and live by.

A person wakes up one day and maintains that he is a rooster. We do not know what he means, and assign him to an insane asylum. But when a person wakes up one day and maintains that he is a human being, we also do not know what he means.

Assuming that the earth were endowed with psychic power, it would raise the question: Who is he—the strange intruder who clips my wings, who trims my gardens? He who cannot live without me and is not quite a part of me?

There are many facets and facts of my being of which I am aware and which remain peripheral and irrelevant to the understanding of my existence. What upsets me most is: What is the meaning of my being?

Mental anguish is occasioned more by the experience or fear of *meaningless* being, of meaningless events, than by the mystery of being, by the absence of being, or by the fear of non-being. The two problems, however, are interdependent. This may be illustrated in dealing with the theme of our inquiry. It is the meaning of man that illumines the being of man, and it is the being of man that both evokes and verifies the meaning of man.

The problem of being and the problem of the meaning of being are not coextensive. In regard to man, the first problem refers to what he is in terms of his own existence, human being as it is; the second refers to what man means in terms larger than himself, being in terms of meaning.

My quest—man's quest—is not for theoretical knowledge about myself. Another discovery of a universal law in nature will not answer my problem. Nor is it simply a striving to extend the length of my life span into an afterlife.

What I look for is not how to gain a firm hold on myself and on life, but primarily how to live a life that would deserve and evoke an eternal Amen. It is not simply a search for certitude (though that is implied in it), but for personal relevance, for a degree of compatibility; not an anchor of being but a direction of being. It is not enough for me to be able to say "I am"; I want to know *who I am,* and in relation to whom I live. It is not enough for me to ask questions; I want to know how to answer the one question that seems to encompass everything I face: What am I here for?

The given datum is man's bewilderment about himself, the fact of his being a problem to himself, of looking for a context to which he belongs and in which to be involved. Man's anguish is in the fear of finding himself locked out of the order of ultimate meaning.

Disregard of the ultimate dimension of human existence is a possible state of mind as long as man finds tranquillity in his dedication to partial objectives. But strange things happen at times to disturb his favorite unawareness, which make it impossible for him not to realize that evasiveness is offensiveness.

In the face of a world full of anguish, of the incoherence of existence, the discovery of our own evasion is a nightmare. When death wipes away a love we have long cherished and taken for granted, when joy deserts us and all common values become vapid, and present moments seem obsolescent, we are bound to realize the peril of evasiveness. Our apprehension lest in winning small prizes we gamble our lives away, throws our souls open to questions we have been trying to avoid.

It is not only the question of how to justify our own existence, but above all, how to justify bringing human beings into the world. If human existence is absurd and miserable, why give birth to children? Do we build cities in order to supply ruins for the archaeologists of a later age? Do we rear children in order to prepare ashes for the outcome of nuclear wars?

But what is there at stake in human life that may be gambled away? It is the meaning of life. In all acts he performs, man raises a claim to meaning. The trees he plants, the tools he invents, are answers to a need or a purpose. In its very essence, consciousness is a dedication to design. Committed to the task of coalescing being with meaning, things with ideas, the mind is driven to ponder whether meaning is something it may invent and invest, something that ought to be attained, or whether there is meaning to existence as it is, to existence as existence, independent of what we may add to it. In other words, is there meaning only to what man does, but none to what he is? Becoming conscious of himself he does not stop at knowing: "I am"; he is driven to know "who" he is. Man may, indeed, be characterized as a subject in quest of a predicate, as a being in quest of a meaning of life, of all of life, not only of particular actions or single episodes which happen now and then.

Meaning denotes a condition that cannot be reduced to a material relation and grasped by the sense organs. Meaning is compatibility with the preciously real; it is, furthermore, that which a fact is for the sake of something else; the pregnancy of an object with value. Life is precious to man. But is it precious to him alone? Or is someone else in need of it?

Imbedded in the mind is a certainty that the state of existence and the state of meaning stand in a relation to each other, that life is assessable in terms of meaning. The will to meaning and the certainty of the legitimacy of our striving to ascertain it are as intrinsically human as the will to live and the certainty of being alive.

54

In spite of failures and frustrations, we continue to be haunted by that irrepressible quest. We can never accept the idea that life is hollow and devoid of meaning.

If at the root of philosophy is not a self-contempt of the mind but the mind's concern for its ultimate surmise, then our aim is to examine in order to know. Seeking contentment in a brilliant subterfuge, we are often ready to embezzle the original surmise. But why should we even care to doubt, if we cease to surmise? Philosophy is what man dares to do with his ultimate surmise of the meaning of existence.

A question to be legitimate must have a chance of being answered. It must entail the beginning or the forecast of an answer if it is to be more than an exclamation of despair. Its "answerability" is indicated in the logical relation of the elements contained in the question. A question such as: Is uranium male or female? is absurd, since the subject stands in no relation to the predicate of the question. We must, therefore, ask whether the subject "human existence" is congruous with the predicate. Is human existence assessable in meaning or are the two concepts incongruous or disparate?

Significant being includes satisfaction of needs and desires, realization of one's capacities as well as a craving transcending these; attainment of beauty, goodness, truth, love, and friendship as well as sensitivities that engender a sense of embarrassment rather than the shelter of self-contentment.

The imperative according to the logic of biology may be: "Eat, drink, and be merry!" Yet a life essentially dedicated to the fulfillment of such an imperative results in depriving human being of all the qualities of being human.

What we are in search of is not meaning for me, an idea to satisfy my conscience, but rather a meaning transcending me, ultimate relevance of human being. There is an appeal to which human being is exposed and occasionally sensitive: an urging for *significant being*. Being as being is intransitive, going-on-ness, continuity; significant being is transitive, going beyond itself, centrifugal.

This, indeed, is the existential paradox. In everydayness the care and solicitude for the self surpass in importance considerations of other goals. Yet, human being without an inkling of a relevance surpassing it is devoid of sense. The self is in need of a meaning which it cannot furnish itself.

The essence of being human

The central question provoked by our description is whether that quest is authentic, rooted in existence, emerging with necessity from our being, or whether it is mere pretension, a defense mechanism, an apologetic device. Is there any sign of our existence not being reducible to just being?

Why be concerned with meaning? Why not be content with satisfaction of desires and needs? Life should be a perfect circle: desire ... pleasure ... desire ... pleasure ... To be concerned with meaning is to go off on a tangent leading to the infinite.

One is, indeed, tempted to dismiss the whole quest for meaning as a passing mood resulting from misguidance in dealing with biological drives, as an imposition by society, or as an artificial superstructure set up by the mind.

According to Freud, the deepest essence of man is the organism's instincts, and their satisfaction man's authentic occupation. However, what is defined here relates to bios (life); it does not relate to existence, which embraces both bios and being human. The vital drives of food, sex, and power, as well as the mental functions aimed at satisfying them, are as characteristic of animals as they are of man. Being human is a characteristic of a being who faces the question: *After satisfaction, what?* The circle of need and satisfaction, of desire and pleasure, is too narrow for the fullness of his existence. Bios, or life, requires satisfaction; existence requires appreciation. Satisfaction is a sensory experience bringing about an end to a desire. Appreciation is an imponderable experience, an opening up, the beginning of a thirst that knows no final satisfaction.

From the perspective of a philosophy of satisfaction, the quest for significant being, which assumes that complete satisfaction is not desirable or conceivable or even possible, must be regarded as a perversion. Yet the logic of being human insists that man's total existence is pledged to the truth that the quest for significant being is the heart of existence.

We do not crave that quest; we find ourselves involved in it. There is no planning, no initiative on our part to embark upon it. There are only moments of finding ourselves in it.

Animals are content when their needs are satisfied; man insists not only on being satisfied but also on being able to satisfy, on being a need not simply on having needs. Personal needs come and go, but one anxiety remains: Am I needed? There is no human being who has not been moved by that anxiety.

It is a most significant fact that man is not sufficient to himself, that life is not meaningful to him unless it is serving an end beyond itself, unless it is of value to someone else.

Man is not an all-inclusive end to himself. The second maxim of Kant's, never to use human beings merely as means but to regard them also as ends, only suggests how a person

57

ought to be treated by other people, not how he ought to treat himself. For if a person thinks that he is an end to himself, then he will use others as means. Moreover, if the idea of man as an end is to be taken as a true estimate of his worth, he cannot be expected to sacrifice his life or his interests for the good of someone else or even of a group. He must treat himself the way he expects others to treat him. Why should even a group or a whole people be worth the sacrifice of one's life? To a person who regards himself as an absolute end a thousand lives will not be worth more than his own life.

Sophisticated thinking may enable him to feign his being sufficient to himself. Yet the way to insanity is paved with such illusions. The feeling of futility that comes with the sense of being useless, of not being needed in the world, is the most common cause of psychoneurosis. The only way to avoid despair is to be a need rather than an end. Happiness, in fact, may be defined as the certainty of being needed. But who is in need of man?

The first answer that comes to mind is a social one—man's purpose is to serve society or mankind. The ultimate worth of a person would then be determined by his usefulness to others, by the efficiency of his social work. Yet, in spite of his instrumentalist atttiude, man expects others to take him not for what he may mean to them but as a being valuable in himself. Even he who does not regard himself as an absolute end rebels against being treated as a means to an end, as subservient to other men. The rich, the men of the world want to be loved for their own sake, for their essence, whatever it may mean, not for their achievements or possessions. Nor do the old and sick expect help because of what they may give us in return. Who needs the old, the incurably sick, the maintenance of whom is a drain on the treasury of the state? It is, moreover, obvious that such service does not claim all one's life and can therefore not be the ultimate answer to his quest of meaning for life as a whole. Man has more to give than what other men are able or willing to accept. To say that life could consist of care for others, of incessant service to the world, would be a vulgar boast. What we are able to bestow upon others is usually less and rarely more than a tithe.

There are alleys in the soul where man walks alone, ways that do not lead to society, a world of privacy that shrinks from the public eye. Life comprises not only arable, productive land, but also mountains of dreams, an underground of sorrow, towers of yearning, which can hardly be utilized to the last for the good of society, unless man be converted into a machine in which every screw must serve a function or be removed. It is a profiteering state which, trying to exploit the individual, asks all of man for itself.

And if society as embodied in the state should prove to be corrupt and my effort to cure its evil unavailing, would my life as an individual have been totally void of meaning? If society should decide to reject my services and even place me in solitary confinement, so that I would surely die without being able to bequeath any benefit to the world I love, would I then feel compelled to end my life?

Human existence cannot derive its ultimate meaning from society, because society itself is in need of meaning. It is as legitimate to ask: Is mankind needed? as it is to ask: Am I needed?

Humanity begins in the individual man, just as history takes its rise from a singular event. It is always one man at a time whom we keep in mind when we pledge: "with mal-

59

ice toward none, with charity for all" or when trying to fulfill: "Love thy neighbor as thyself." The term "mankind," which in biology denotes the human species, has an entirely different meaning in the realm of ethics and religion. Here mankind is not conceived as a species, as an abstract concept, stripped from its concrete reality, but as an abundance of specific individuals; as a community of persons rather than as a herd of nondescripts.

It is true that the good of all counts more than the good of one, but it is the concrete individual who lends meaning to the human race. We do not think that a human being is valuable because he is a member of the race; it is rather the opposite: the human race is valuable because it is composed of human beings.

Though we are dependent on society as well as on the air that sustains us, and though other men compose the system of relations in which the curve of our actions takes its course, it is as individuals that we are beset with desires, fears, and hopes, challenged, called upon, and endowed with the power of will and a spark of responsibility.

But who is in need of man? Nature? Do the mountains stand in need of our poems? Would the stars fade away if astronomers ceased to exist? The earth can get along without the aid of the human species. Nature is replete with opportunity to satisfy all our needs except one—the need of being needed. Within its unbroken silence man is like the middle of a sentence and all his theories are like dots indicating his isolation within his own self.

Unlike all other needs, the need of being needed is a striving to give rather than to obtain satisfaction. It is a desire to satisfy a transcendent desire, a craving to satisfy a craving.

All needs are one-sided. When hungry we are in need of food, yet food is not in need of being consumed. Things of beauty attract our minds; we feel the need of perceiving them, yet they are not in need of being perceived by us. It is in such one-sidedness that most of living is imprisoned. Examine an obtuse mind, and you will find that it is dominated by an effort to cut reality to the measure of the ego, as if the world existed for the sake of pleasing one's ego. Everyone of us entertains more relations with things than with people, and even in dealings with people we behave toward them as if they were things, tools, means to be used for our own selfish ends. How rarely do we face a person as a person! We are all dominated by the desire to appropriate and to own. Only a free person knows that the true meaning of existence is experienced in giving, in endowing, in meeting a person face to face, in fulfilling higher needs.

All our experiences are needs, dissolving when the needs are fulfilled. But the truth is, our existence, too, is a need. We are such stuff as needs are made of, and our little life is rounded by a will. Lasting in our life is neither passion nor delight, neither joy nor pain, but the answer to a need. The lasting in us is not our will to live. There is a need for our lives, and in living we satisfy it. Lasting is not our desire, but our answer to that need, an agreement not an impulse. Our needs are temporal, but our being needed is lasting.

Of all phenomena which take place in the soul, desires have the highest rate of mortality. Like aquatic plants, they grow and live in the waters of oblivion, impatient to vanish. Inherent in desire is the intention to expire; it asserts itself in order to be quenched, and in attaining satisfaction it comes to an end, singing its own dirge.

Such suicidal intention is not vested in all human acts. Thoughts, concepts, laws, theories are born with the intent to endure. A problem, for example, does not cease to be relevant when its solution is achieved. Inherent in reason is the intention to endure, a striving to comprehend the valid, to form concepts the cogency of which goes on forever. It is, therefore, not in pondering about ideas but in surveying one's inner life and discovering the graveyard of needs and desires, once fervently cherished, that we become intimately aware of the temporality of existence.

Yet there is a curious ambiguity in the way in which this awareness is entertained. For, even though there is nothing man is more intimately sure of than the temporality of existence, he is rarely resigned to the role of a mere undertaker of desires.

Walking upon a rock that is constantly crumbling away behind every step and anticipating the inevitable abruption that will end his walk, man cannot restrain his bitter yearning to know whether life is nothing but a series of momentary physiological and mental processes, actions, and forms of behavior, a flow of vicissitudes, desires, and sensations, running like grains through an hourglass, marking time only once and always vanishing.

He wonders whether, at bottom, life is not like the face of the sundial, outliving all shadows that rotate upon its surface. Is life nothing but an agglomeration of facts, unrelated to one another—chaos camouflaged by illusion?

There is not a soul on this earth which, however vaguely or rarely, has not realized that life is dismal unless mirrored in something which is lasting. We are all in search of a conviction that there is something that is worth the toil of living.

There is not a soul which has not felt a craving to know of something that outlasts life, strife, and agony.

Helpless and incongruous is man with all his craving, with his tiny candles in the mist. Is it his will to be good that would heal the wounds of his soul, his fright and frustration? It is too obvious that his will is a door to a house divided against itself, that his good intentions, after enduring for a while, touch the mud of vanity, like the horizon of his life which some day will touch the grave. Is there anything beyond the horizon of our good intentions?

Despair, the sense of the futility of living, is an attitude, the reality of which no psychologist will question. But just as real is our fear of despair, our horror of futility. Human life and despair seem to be incompatible. Man is a being in search of significant being, of ultimate meaning of existence.

Ultimate meaning implies not only that man is part of a whole, an adjunct to greatness, but an answer to a question, the satisfaction of a need; not only that man is tolerated but also that he is needed, precious, indispensable. Life is precious to man. Is it precious to man alone?

The being of the being human is not the being of a neutral fact, "just being," but rather a relationship of human being to meaning. Since being human is a necessity of human being, a distinction must be made between two ways of reflection.

With other objects it is possible to reflect on their pure being, unrelated to meaning, thrown into the world. With humanity, it is impossible to reflect about its being without regard to its meaning. We can think of human being only in terms of meaning: it is either devoid of, or indicative of, ultimate meaning.

63

Just as reasoning about and exploring the reality of the world are inconceivable without being in the world, reflecting about meaning is inconceivable without being involved in meaning. We are concerned because we are involved. Meaning, therefore, is more than a logical presupposition of our reflection; it is meaning that drives us to think about meaning.

Reflecting about the infinite universe, we could perhaps afford to resign ourselves to the trivial position of being a nonentity. However, pondering over our reflection, we discover that we are carried and surrounded by the mystery of meaning. Man is a fountain of immense meaning, not merely a drop in the ocean of being.

The problem will not be solved by declaring our claim to significant being to be a meaningless pretension, for the fact of declaring that claim to be an empty pretension contains a claim to meaning. The declaration itself claims to be significant thinking, and significant thinking is meaningless without significant being. Asking any question, even, "Is this quest for meaning an empty pretension?" presupposes the meaningfulness of life and the value of the search for truth to man's life.

The care for significant being is inherent in being human—it is strong, elementary, provocative, dwelling in every heart—whereas the tendency to question the claim to the possibility of significant being is derivative. Important as its function is to unmask extravagant, absurd, or superstitious claims, its power remains within the limits of reason. Its onslaught can suppress or severely weaken but never destroy with its weapon of reason a claim that surpasses reason. No argument will avail against the power of biological instincts; no skepticism or cynicism can destroy a claim which has its roots in the power of being human.

The quest for ultimate relevance of being is a response to a requiredness of existence: not something derived from human nature, but something that constitutes the nature of being human. Truth would cease to be valuable if the quest for ultimate relevance of being human were irrelevant. If anxiety about supreme significance—the driving force of all achievement in philosophy and art—is to be considered an absurdity, then to be human would mean to be mad. The question, however, would be: What is more deserving of being called mad, the search for significance or the condemnation of such anxiety as madness? Would the soul of humanity be cured by removing its cause and by declaring that the search for the venerable is a misguided and absurd endeavor, that the quest of meaning is meaningless, that the questions asked are irrelevant?

It is beyond the power of the mind to prove that being human is a fact of undeniable validity. Man cannot verify his humanity in terms that would transcend his existence. Indeed, being human can only be grasped in human terms, and its validity remains contingent upon the validity of human terms. Man cannot prove transcendent meaning; he is a manifestation of transcendent meaning.

The human species is too powerful, too dangerous, to be a mere toy or a freak. It undoubtedly represents something unique in the great body of the universe: a growth, as it were, an abnormal mass of tissue, which not only began to interact with other parts but also, to some degree, was able to modify their status. What is its nature and function? Is it malignant,

65

a tumor, or is it supposed to serve as a brain of the universe?

The human species shows at times symptoms of being malignant and, if its growth remains unchecked, it may destroy the entire body for the sake of its expansion. In terms of astronomical time, our civilization is in its infancy. The expansion of human power has hardly begun, and what man is going to do with his power may either save or destroy our planet.

The earth may be of small significance within the infinite universe. But if it is of some significance, man holds the key to it.

The relevance of human being depends upon the truth of being human. The truth of being human discloses that man is a being involved in a relationship to meaning, a relationship rooted in the human situation, not the product of wishful thinking.

The secret of being human is care for meaning. Man is not his own meaning, and if the essence of being human is concern for transcendent meaning, then man's secret lies in openness to transcendence. Existence is interspersed with suggestions of transcendence, and openness to transcendence is a constitutive element of being human.

Such is the structure of our situation that human being without an intuition of meaning cannot long remain a fact; it soon stares us in the face as a nightmare.

Indeed, the concern for meaning of human being is what constitutes the truth of being human. Its ontological relevance is rooted in the very being of man, since human being devoid of the possibility of being human is an absurdity. Our attempts to formulate it are awkward, but the necessity to be concerned for it is authentic.

Being and meaning

We have defined man's quest for meaning as an effort to understand the self (as well as humanity) in terms larger than the self, as a striving to attain an inkling of ultimate relevance of the human being. Man cannot be understood in his own terms. He can only be understood, we repeat, in terms of a larger context. Our problem, now, is: What is the context of man, in terms of which he can be ultimately understood?

Is human being to be understood as an aspect of anonymous, neutral Being? Or is the human a mode of being which seeks to surpass sheer being? Is human being to be regarded as an example of what is latently present in anonymous Being? Or is human being a breakthrough to what is meant by being?

The quest of the meaning of being is a quest for that which surpasses being, expressing insufficiency of sheer being. Meaning and being are, as said above, not coextensive. Meaning is a primary category not reducible to being as such. There may be meaning to that which is not yet, as there may be being destructive of meaning. Just as we are aware of being and of coming into being, we are aware of meaning and of coming into meaning.

Existence does not receive its meaning from the realm of being, because being-itself is less than being human. The human is not derived from being; although it may vanish within it.

The mandates and necessities of being do not exhaust the depth of being human. Man's vocation is not acceptance of being, but relating it to meaning; and his unique problem is not how to come into being, but how to come into meaning.

The thirst, the quest, the homelessness breaking forth in the fullness of being, is it not a cry for relatedness to what is beyond being? If self-insufficiency is inherent in human being, is it not a sign that being as such is not the ultimate, all-embracing category for the understanding of man?

Human being is the cradle of man's coming into meaning, and its preciousness remains the prerequisite of all values. Yet sheer being does not generate goodness or beauty. Unguided, unfathered being may become vicious and uncouth. It is only despair that claims: the task of man is to let the world be. It is self-deception to assume that man can ever be an innocent spectator. To be human is to be involved, *nolens volens,* to act and to react, to wonder and to respond. For man, to be is to play a part in a cosmic drama, knowingly or unknowingly.

Being and living

In speaking about human being we have in mind a being very much alive. Living is a situation, the content of which is much richer than the concept of being. The term "human being" is apt to suggest that the human is but a mode of being in general, with the emphasis placed on being. Since the power of a term easily determines the image of what we undertake to explore, we must always keep in mind that it is the *living* man we seek to understand when we speak of the human being: human being as human living.

Man's most important problem is not being but living. To live means to be at the crossroads. There are many forces and drives within the self. What direction to take? is a question we face again and again.

Who am I? A mere chip from the block of being? Am I not both the chisel and the marble? Being and foreseeing? Being and bringing into being?

A more adequate formulation of our problem would be in asking: What is the context to which we must relate the *living* man?

A major difference between ontological and biblical thinking is that the first seeks to relate the human being to a transcendence called being as such, whereas the second, realizing that human being is more than being, that human being is living being, seeks to relate man to divine living, to a transcendence called the living God.

The cardinal difference underlying these two approaches is that the first, or ontological, approach accepts being as the ultimate, whereas the biblical approach accepts *living as the ultimately real*. The first seeks to understand living in terms of being, the second seeks to understand being in terms of living.

According to the second approach, we cannot solve the problem of the ultimate context of man by positing being as such as the ultimate, because this would be merely a verbal solution of the problem. To man, whose chief attribute is life, being deprived of life and purpose, mere inorganic subsistence is in truth non-being.

The dilemma faced by the living man is whether the ultimate transcendence is alive or not alive. Making the option for the ultimacy of being as being, the status of man as a living being becomes precarious. If the ultimate is sheer being, the human living has nothing to relate himself to as living. He can only relate himself to nothing. What surrounds him is a void where all life is left behind, where values and thoughts are devoid of all relevance and reference. Facing being as being, man "discovers himself confronted by the Nothingness, the possible impossibility of his existence." Man may see himself between "thrownness" at one end and death at the other and so maintain: Out of Nothingness I came and into Nothingness I shall return. My existence draws its reality from Nothing and is destined to be dissolved in Nothing.

The cardinal error is to take being for granted, to regard being as ultimate, as absolute transcendence. Being as being is vague, inconceivable, something not to be enclosed in any mental concept. Yet, at least intellectually, we transcend being, by questioning it, by asking: How is being possible?

Is being to be taken as the ultimate theme of thinking? The fact that there is being at all is as puzzling as the question of the origin of being. Any ontology that disregards the wonder and mystery of being is guilty of suppressing the genuine amazement of the mind, and of taking being for granted. It is true that being's coming-into-being "can neither be thought nor uttered." Yet a fact does not cease to be fact because of its transcending the limits of thought and expression. Indeed, the very theme of ontology, being *as* being "can neither be thought nor uttered."

The acceptance of the ultimacy of being is a *petitio principii;* it mistakes a problem for a solution. The supreme and ultimate issue is not *being* but the *mystery of being*. Why is there being at all instead of nothing? We can never think of any being without conceiving the possibility of its not being. We are always exposed to the presence as well as to the absence of being. Thus, what we face is a pair of concepts rather than one ultimate concept. Both concepts are transcended by the mystery of being.

The biblical man does not begin with being, but with the surprise of being. The biblical man is free of what may be called the ontocentric predicament. Being is not *all* to him. He is not enchanted by the given, granting the alternative, namely, the annihilation of the given. To Parmenides, not-being is inconceivable ("Nothingness is not possible"); to the biblical mind, nothingness or the end of being is not impossible. Realizing the contingency of being, it could never identify being with ultimate reality. Being is neither self-evident nor self-explanatory. Being points to the question of how being is possible. The act of bringing being into being, creation, stands higher in the ladder of problems than being. Creation is not a transparent concept. But is the concept of being as being distinguished by lucidity? Creation is a mystery; being as being an abstraction.

The mind dares to go behind being in asking about the source of being. It is true that the concept of that source implies being, yet it is also true that a Being that calls a reality into being is endowed with the kind of being that transcends mysteriously all conceivable being. Thus, whereas ontology asks about *being as being,* theology asks about *being as creation,* about being as a divine act. From the perspective of *continuous creation,* there is no being as being; there is only *continuous coming-into-being.* Being is both action and event.*

The universe, Being itself, cannot offer an answer to the question of the meaning of the universe, or the meaning of being, since the question seeks to assess being in terms other than being, in terms exceeding the universe. The question refers to transcendence of being; it affirms what is beyond,

* See A. J. Heschel, *The Prophets* (New York, 1962), pp. 263f.

over, and above being. In asking it, we leave the level of logical and strictly verifiable thinking and climb to the level of mystery. Such a step is one which logically we must not take; it transcends the boundaries of legitimate logic. Yet in spite of all warnings insisting and proving that the question is meaningless, man will never cease to raise it. The question affirms its own validity. Science cannot silence him, the power of logic cannot permanently suppress it. Indeed, in giving up the anxiety for meaning, man would cease to be human; logical positivism's gain would be humanity's loss.

There are many reasons against the search for meaning, yet just as no theory about the harmfulness of breathing will cause man to abstain from breathing, no theory about irrelevance of the question of meaning will eradicate man's concern for it.

Who is man's meaning?

We have questioned the adequacy of the formulation, "What is man?" But should we not equally attack the formulation, "What is the meaning of human being?" as a willful reduction of the meaning of being a person to a thing or an idea? The very formulation "What is the meaning of ..." is obviously not derived from the realm of thinghood, and as such excludes from the beginning the possibility of finding an answer in the realm of thinghood. Our ideas of hot and cold are abstracted from experiences in the realm of things. The meaning of human being, however, is not a property like hot and cold which can be experienced through sense perception. Nor is an answer to be found in abstractions or Platonic ideas, since the problem we are concerned with arises out of the full situation of the living man, embracing the dynamics and concrete reality of his individual existence, including the ultimate relevance of his thinking as well as the ideas and abstractions he comprehends.

On the other hand, to assume that the meaning we are in search of, namely, the meaning of being a person, is in the realm of personhood would be a tautology. The difficulty, then, lies in the fact that only two realms are accessible to us, thinghood and personhood, and what we are in search of either seems to be a figment of the imagination or is to be found in, belongs to, or is another realm.

Ultimate meaning as an idea is no answer to our anxiety. Humanity is more than an intellectual structure; it is a personal reality. The cry for meaning is a cry for ultimate relationship, for ultimate belonging. It is a cry in which all pretensions are abandoned. Are we alone in the wilderness of time, alone in the dreadfully marvelous universe, of which we are a part and where we feel forever like strangers? Is there a Presence to live by? A Presence worth living for, worth dying for? Is there a way of living in the Presence? Is there a way of living compatible with the Presence?

As said above, the universe does not reveal its secret to us, and what it says is not expressed in the language of man. The ultimate meaning of man is not to be derived from ultimate being. Ultimate being is devoid of any relationship to particular beings, and unless meaning is related to me, I am not related to meaning.

Man is in need of meaning, but if ultimate meaning is not in need of man, and he cannot relate himself to it, then ultimate meaning is meaningless to him. As a one-sided relationship, as a reaching-out or searching-for, the meeting of man and meaning would remain a goal beyond man's reach.

73

Meaning in quest of man

The Greeks formulated the search of meaning as man in search of a thought; the Hebrews formulated the search of meaning as God's thought (or concern) in search of man. The meaning of existence is not naturally given; it is not an endowment but an art. It rather depends on whether we respond or refuse to respond to God who is in search of man; it is either fulfilled or missed.

Man's anxiety about meaning is not a question, an impulse, but an answer, a response to a challenge.

The Bible maintains that the question about God is a question of God. If the Lord did not ask the question, in vain would be the labor of those who deal with it. Man is being called upon, challenged, and solaced. God is in search of man, and life is something that requires an answer. History is above all a question, a fathoming, a probing, a testing.

The primary topic, then, of biblical thinking is not man's knowledge of God but rather man's being known by God, man's being an object of divine knowledge and concern. This is why the great puzzle was: Why should God, the Creator of heaven and earth, be concerned with man? Why should the deeds of puny man be relevant enough to affect the life of God?

> Can a man be profitable unto God?
> Or can he that is wise be profitable unto Him?
> Is it any advantage to the Almighty, that thou art righteous?
> Or is it gain to Him, that thou makest thy ways blameless?
> Job 22:2–3

God takes man seriously. He enters a direct relationship with man, namely, *a covenant,* to which not only man but also God is committed. In his ultimate confrontation and crises the biblical man knows not only God's eternal mercy and justice but also *God's commitment to man.* Upon this sublime fact rests the meaning of history and the glory of human destiny.

Essential to biblical religion is the *awareness of God's interest in man,* the awareness of a covenant, of a responsibility that lies on Him as well as on us. Our task is to concur with His interest, to carry out His vision of our task. God is in need of man for the attainment of His ends, and religion, as biblical tradition understands it, is a way of serving these ends, of which we are in need, even though we may not be aware of them, ends which we must learn to feel the need of.

Life is a *partnership* of God and man; God is not detached from or indifferent to our joys and griefs. Authentic vital needs of man's body and soul are a divine concern. This is why human life is holy. God is a partner and a partisan in man's struggle for justice, peace, love, and beauty, and it is because of His being in need of man that He entered a covenant with him for all time, a mutual bond embracing God and man, a relationship to which God, not alone man, is committed.

Meaning beyond the mystery

Ever since Schleiermacher it has been customary in considering the nature of religion to start with the human self and to characterize religion as a feeling of dependence, reverence, etc. What is overlooked is the unique aspect of religious consciousness of being a recipient, of being exposed, overwhelmed by a presence which surpasses our ability to feel.

What characterizes the religious man is faith in God's transitive concern for humanity, faith in God's commitment to man, in terms of which he seeks to shape his life and attempts to find sense in history.

Facing the world must not be equated with passivity or surrender. It means not to mistake the perceptible for the unutterable. It means being in touch with sheer being.

The world is not related to us, and there is a whole realm in the inner life of man which is not related to the world. Man and the world have a mystery in common: the mystery of being dependent upon meaning, which is not simply given in sheer being.

What we produce has meaning in relation to us who produce it. It is the sheer being of the universe that calls forth the question about meaning. It is in conjunction with the universe that the ultimate question is evolved.

The tragedy of modern man is that he thinks alone. He broods about his own affairs rather than thinking for all being. He has moved out of the realm of God's creation into the realm of man's manipulation.

This seems to be the malady of man: *His normal consciousness is a state of oblivion,* a state of suspended sensitivity. As a result, we see only camouflage and concealment. We do not understand what we do; we do not see what we face.

Is there a meaning beyond all conventional meanings? The Greeks discovered rational structure of the given, yet beyond the given and the rational they sensed dark mystery—irrational fate or necessity that stood over and above men and gods, a mysterious power which filled even Zeus with fear.

We are so impressed by our intellectual power that we deny any presence lying beyond our power. What we define *is*; what we cannot define *is not* and cannot be.

To the biblical man was given the understanding that beyond all mystery is meaning. God is neither plain meaning nor just mystery. God is meaning that transcends mystery, meaning that mystery alludes to, meaning that speaks through mystery.

The mystery is not a synonym for the unknown, but rather a term for a meaning which stands in relation to God.

Being is a mystery, being is concealment, but there is meaning beyond the mystery. The meaning beyond the mystery seeks to come to expression. The destiny of human being is to articulate what is concealed. The divine seeks to be disclosed in the human.

Silence hovers over all the mountain peaks. The world is aflame with grandeur. Each flower is an outpouring of love. Each being speaks for itself. Man alone can speak for all beings. Human living alone enacts the mystery as a drama.

Transcendent meaning

The awareness of transcendent meaning comes with the sense of the ineffable. The *imperative of awe* is its certificate of evidence, a universal response which we experience *not* because we desire to, but because we are stunned and cannot brave the impact of the sublime. It is a meaning wrapped in mystery.

It is not by analogy or inference that we become aware of it. It is rather sensed as something immediately given, logically and psychologically prior to judgment, to the assimilation of subject matter to mental categories; a universal insight into an objective aspect of reality, of which all men are at all times capable; not the froth of ignorance but the climax of thought, indigenous to the climate that prevails at the summit of intellectual endeavor.

It is a cognitive insight, since the awareness it evokes adds to our deeper understanding of the world.

Transcendent meaning is a meaning that surpasses our comprehension. A finite meaning that would fit perfectly our categories would not be an ultimate explanation, since it would still call for further explanation and would be an answer unrelated to our ultimate question. A finite meaning that claims to be an ultimate answer is specious. The assumption, for example, that the pursuit of knowledge, the enjoyment of beauty, or sheer being is an end in itself, is a principle we may utter, not a truth man can live by. Tell man that he is an end in himself, and his answer will be despair. The finite has beauty but no grandeur; it may be pleasing but not redeeming.

Finite meaning is a thought we comprehend; infinite meaning is a thought that comprehends us; finite meaning we absorb; infinite meaning we encounter. Finite meaning has clarity; infinite meaning has depth. Finite meaning we comprehend with analytical reason; to infinite meaning we respond in awe. Infinite meaning is uncomfortable, not compatible with our categories. It is not to be grasped as though it were something in the world which appeared before us. Rather it is that in which the world appears to us. It is not an object—not a self-subsistent, timeless idea or value; it is a presence.

There is no insight into transcendent meaning without the premise of wonder and the premise of awe. We say "premise" because wonder and awe are not emotions, but are cognitive acts involving value judgments.

The sense of wonder is not the mist in our eyes or the fog in our words. Wonder, or radical amazement, is a way of going beyond what is given in thing and thought, refusing to take anything for granted, to regard anything as final. It is our honest response to the grandeur and mystery of reality, our confrontation with that which transcends the given.

It would be a contradiction in terms to assume that the attainment of transcendent meaning consists in comprehending a notion. Transcendence can never be an object of possession or of comprehension. Yet man can relate himself and be engaged to it. He must know how to court meaning in order to be engaged to it. Love of ultimate meaning is not self-centered but rather a concern to transcend the self. Moreover, ideas, formulas, or doctrines are generalities, impersonal, timeless, and as such they remain incongruous with the essential mode of human existence which is concrete, personal, here and now. Transcendent meaning must not be reduced to an object of acknowledgment, to saying "yes" to an idea. The experience of a meaning is an experience of vital involvement, not having an idea in mind but living within a spirit surpassing the mind; not an experience of a private reference of meaning, but sharing a dimension open to all human beings. We meet in a stillness of significance, disclosing a fellowship of being related to a concern for meaning. The longing for such experience is part of man's ultimate vocation. In this longing, he acts, it seems, for all men. Any meaning, therefore, relevant only to one man is no answer to any man. The relationship of a human being to ultimate meaning can never be conceived as possession.

Ultimate meaning is not grasped once and for all in the form of a timeless idea, acquired once and for all, securely preserved in conviction. It is not simply given. It comes upon us as an intimation that comes and goes. What is left behind

79

is a memory, and a commitment to that memory. Our words do not describe it, our tools do not wield it. But sometimes it seems as if our very being were its description, its secret tool.

The anchor of meaning resides in an abyss, deeper than the reach of despair. Yet the abyss is not infinite; its bottom may suddenly be discovered within the confines of a human heart or under the debris of mighty doubts.

This may be the vocation of man: to say "Amen" to being and to the Author of being; to live in defiance of absurdity, notwithstanding futility and defeat; to attain faith in God even in spite of God.

Chapter five

Manipulation and appreciation

The sense of meaning is not born in ease and sloth. It comes after bitter trials, disappointments in the glitters, founderings, strandings. It is the marrow from the bone. There is no manna in our wilderness.

Thought is not bred apart from experience or from inner surroundings. Thinking is living, and no thought is bred in an isolated cell in the brain. No thought is an island.

We think with all faculties; our entire living is involved in our thinking. Thus our way of thinking is affected by our way of living, and contemplation is the distillation of one's entire existence. Thinking is a summing up of the truth of our own living.

The manner in which I relate myself to the being of this pen, paper, and desk affects my way of reflecting on ultimate issues.

Ultimately there is no power to narcissistic, self-indulgent thinking. Authentic thinking originates in an encounter with the world. We think not only in concepts; we think *in* the world. Thinking echoes man's total relationship to the world.

Human being is both being in the world and living in the world. Living involves responsible understanding of one's role in relation to all other beings. For living is not being in itself, by itself, but living off the world, affecting, exploiting, consuming, comprehending, deriving, depriving.

How does man identify or regard the world? What is the face of the world in the eyes of man? How does he relate himself to the world?

There are two primary ways in which man relates himself to the world that surrounds him: *manipulation* and *appreciation*. In the first way he sees in what surrounds him things to be handled, forces to be managed, objects to be put to use. In the second way he sees in what surrounds him things to be acknowledged, understood, valued or admired.

It is the hand that creates the tools for the purpose of manipulation (*manus* means hand), and it is the ear and the eye by which we attain appreciation. Following the example of the hand, sight, hearing, and particularly speech, become tools of manipulation. Man begins to use his ear and his eye in order to exploit; his words become tools.

Fellowship depends upon appreciation, while manipulation is the cause of alienation: objects and I apart, things stand dead, and I am alone. What is more decisive: a life of manipulation distorts the image of the world. Reality is equated with availability: what I can manipulate is, what I cannot manipulate is not. A life of manipulation is the death of transcendence.

A premise of significant being is full and grateful acceptance of one's own being. Perceptions, moments of insight, the privilege of being present at the unfolding of time—who has the right to ask for more?

Acceptance is appreciation, and the high value of appreciation is such that to appreciate appreciation seems to be the fundamental prerequisite for survival. Mankind will not die for lack of information; it may perish for lack of appreciation.

Biblical religion is in a sense rebellion against the tyranny of things, a revolt against confinement in the world. Man is given the choice of being lost in the world or of being a partner in mastering and redeeming the world.

Man is from the beginning not submerged in nature nor totally derived from it. He must not surrender to the impersonal, to the earth, to being as such. Surrendering, he gradually obliterates himself. Turning beast, he becomes a cannibal. He is not simply in nature. He is free and capable of rising above nature, of conquering and controlling it. In the Prometheus myth man steals fire against the will of the gods; in the Bible man has the divine mandate to rise above nature. In this spirit, it is said in a Midrash that God taught Adam the art of making fire.

According to the Bible, the conquest of nature is a means to an end; man's mastery is a privilege that must be neither misunderstood nor abused.

Disavowal of transcendence

Prior to the discovery of nature's submissiveness to the power of man, man is clearly aware that nature does not belong to him. The awareness of nature's otherness precedes the awareness of nature's availability. However, as a result of letting the drive for power dominate existence, man is bound to lose his sense for nature's otherness. Nature becomes a utensil, an object to be used. The world ceases to be that which is and becomes that which is available.

It is a submissive world that modern man is in the habit of sensing, and he seems content with the riches of thinghood.

83

Space is the limit of his ambitions, and there is little he desires besides it. Correspondingly, man's consciousness recedes more and more in the process of reducing his status to that of a consumer and manipulator. He has enclosed himself in the availability of things, with the shutters down and no sight of what is beyond availability.

His way of thinking tends to flatten things. He deals with them as if they had no depth, as if the world had only two dimensions. He has developed a sense of power, a sense of beauty; he knows how to use the forces of matter, how to enjoy the beauty of nature. Intellectually he knows that the universe is not here for his sake; not here to please his ego. Practically, however, he acts as if the purpose of the universe were to satisfy his needs.

Exclusive manipulation results in the dissolution of awareness of all transcendence. Promise becomes a pretext, God becomes a symbol, truth a fiction, loyalty tentative, the holy a mere convention. Man's very existence devours all transcendence. Instead of facing the grandeur of the cosmos, he explains it away; instead of beholding, he takes a picture; instead of hearing a voice, he tapes it. He does not see what he is able to face.

There is a suspension of man's sense of the holy. His mind is becoming a wall instead of being a door open to what is larger than the scope of his comprehension. He locks himself out of the world by reducing all reality to mere things and all relationship to mere manipulation.

Transcendence is not an article of faith. It is what we come upon immediately when standing face to face with reality.

For the world of stable objects which we seek to explore

and to control is not *all* of reality. The perceptibility of things is not the end of their being. Their surface is available to our tools, their depth is immune to our inquisitiveness.

Things are both available and immune. We penetrate their physical givenness, we cannot intuit their secret. We measure what they exhibit, we know how they function, but we also know that we do not know what they are, what they stand for, what they imply. A tree we describe as a woody perennial plant having a single main axis or stem (trunk) commonly exceeding ten feet in height. Is that all there is in the tree I face?

Existence and expediency

Man is naturally self-centered, and he is inclined to regard expediency as the supreme standard for what is right and wrong. However, we must not convert an inclination into an axiom that just as man's perceptions cannot operate outside time and space, so his motivations cannot operate outside expediency; that man can never transcend his own self. The most fatal trap into which thinking may fall is the equation of existence and expediency.

Ultimate reliance on the self-regulating force of class and national interests, the Golden Calf of the modern age, is wishful thinking. Who is wise enough to know what his true interests are? Does not the clash of interests that ends in war and mutual extermination prove the folly of ultimate reliance on expediency?

The supremacy of expediency is being refuted by time and truth. Time is an essential dimension of existence defiant of man's power, and truth reigns in supreme majesty, unrivaled,

85

inimitable, and can never be defeated. Man cannot fabricate it but only submit to it. Anteceding man, truth is a prefiguration of transcendence.

Expediency as an absolute is a circle in which man is easily trapped. Where expediency is the limit, existing becomes a cul-de-sac. Authentic existence involves exaltation, sensitivity to the holy, awareness of indebtedness.

Existence without transcendence is a way of living where things become idols and idols become monsters.

Denial of transcendence contradicts the essential truth of being human. Its root can be traced either to stolidity of self-contentment or to superciliousness of contempt, to moods rather than to comprehensive awareness of the totality and mystery of being.

Denial of transcendence which claims to unveil the truth of being is an inner contradiction, since the truth of being is not within being or within our consciousness of being but rather a truth that transcends our being.

Essential to education for being human is to cultivate a sense for the inexpedient, to disclose the fallacy of absolute expediency. God's voice may sound feeble to our conscience. Yet there is a divine cunning in history which seems to prove that the wages of absolute expediency is disaster.

Happiness is not a synonym for self-satisfaction, complacency, or smugness. Self-satisfaction breeds futility and despair. Self-satisfaction is the opiate of fools.

Self-fulfillment is a myth which a noble mind must find degrading. All that is creative in man stems from a seed of endless discontent. New insight begins when satisfaction comes to an end, when all that has been seen, said, or done looks like a distortion.

The aim is the maintenance and fanning of a discontent with our aspirations and achievements, the maintenance and fanning of a craving that knows no satisfaction. Man's true fulfillment depends upon communion with that which transcends him.

We are involved in a paradox. Discontent is a feeling of uneasiness which we should seek to overcome. Yet to eradicate discontent is to turn man into a machine. Let us imagine a state in which all goals have been achieved—disease overcome, poverty eliminated, longevity achieved, urban communities established on Mars and other planets, the moon made a part of our empire. Will bliss have been achieved?

"In this world," said Oscar Wilde, "there are only two tragedies. One is not getting what one wants, and the other is getting it. The last is the real tragedy."

The sense of the ineffable

In our reflection we must go back to where we stand in awe before sheer being, facing the marvel of the moment. The world is not just here. It shocks us into amazement.

Of being itself all we can positively say is: being is ineffable. The heart of being confronts me as enigmatic, incompatible with my categories, sheer mystery. My power of probing is easily exhausted, my words fade, but what I sense is not emptiness but inexhaustible abundance, ineffable abundance. What I face I cannot utter or phrase in language. But the richness of my facing the abundance of being endows me with marvelous reward: a sense of the ineffable.

Being as we know it, the world as we come upon it, stands before us as otherness, remoteness. For all our efforts to exploit or comprehend it, it remains evasive, mysteriously immune. Being is unbelievable.

Our concern with environment cannot be reduced to what can be used, to what can be grasped. Environment includes not only the inkstand and the blotting paper, but also the impenetrable stillness in the air, the stars, the clouds, the quiet passing of time, the wonder of my own being. I am an end as well as a means, and so is the world: an end as well as a means. My view of the world and my understanding of the self determine each other. The complete manipulation of the world results in the complete instrumentalization of the self.

The world presents itself in two ways to me. The world as a thing I own, the world as a mystery I face. What I own is a trifle, what I face is sublime. I am careful not to waste what I own; I must learn not to miss what I face.

We manipulate what is available on the surface of the world; we must also stand in awe before the mystery of the world. We objectify Being but we also are present at Being in wonder, in radical amazement.

All we have is a sense of awe and radical amazement in the face of a mystery that staggers our ability to sense it.

No one can ridicule the stars, or poke fun at an atomic explosion. No one can debunk the man who committed suicide in order to call the attention of the world to the Nazi atrocities.

Awe is more than an emotion; it is a way of understanding, insight into a meaning greater than ourselves. The beginning of awe is wonder, and the beginning of wisdom is awe.

Awe is an intuition for the dignity of all things, a realization that things not only are what they are but also stand, however remotely, for something supreme. Awe is a sense for the transcendence, for the reference everywhere to mystery beyond all things. It enables us to perceive in the world intimations of the divine, to sense in small things the beginning of infinite significance, to sense the ultimate in the common and the simple; to feel in the rush of the passing the stillness of the eternal. What we cannot comprehend by analysis, we become aware of in awe.

Faith is not belief, an assent to a proposition; faith is attachment to transcendence, to the meaning beyond the mystery.

Knowledge is fostered by curiosity; wisdom is fostered by awe. *Awe precedes faith; it is the root of faith.* We must be guided by awe to be worthy of faith.

Forfeit your sense of awe, let your conceit diminish your ability to revere, and the universe becomes a market place for you. The loss of awe is the avoidance of insight. A return to reverence is the first prerequisite for a revival of wisdom, for the discovery of the world as an allusion to God.

Presence

In his great vision Isaiah perceives the voice of the seraphim even before he hears the voice of the Lord. What is it that the seraphim reveal? "Holy, holy, holy is the Lord of hosts; the whole earth is full of His glory."

Holy, holy, holy—indicate the transcendence and distance of God. The whole earth is full of this glory—the immanence or presence of God. The outwardness of the world communicates something of the indwelling greatness of God.

The glory is neither an aesthetic nor a physical quality. It is sensed in grandeur, but it is more than grandeur. It is *a presence or the effulgence of a presence.*

The whole earth is full of His glory, but we do not perceive it; it is within our reach but beyond our grasp. And still it is not entirely unknown to us.

In English the phrase that a person has "a presence" is hard to define. There are people whose being here and now is felt, even though they do not display themselves in action and speech. They have "presence." Other people may be here all the time, but no one will be aware of their presence. Of a person whose outwardness communicates something of his indwelling power or greatness, whose soul is radiant and conveys itself without words, we say he has presence.

Standing face to face with the world, we often sense a presence which surpasses our ability to comprehend. The world is too much for us. It is crammed with marvel. There is a glory, an aura, that lies about all beings, a spiritual setting of reality.

To the religious man it is as if things stood with their backs to him, their faces turned to God, as if the glory of things consisted in their being an object of divine care.

Being is both presence and absence. God had to conceal His presence in order to bring the world into being. He had to make His absence possible in order to make room for the world's presence. Coming into being brought along denial and defiance, absence, oblivion, and resistance.

Pathos

By being we mean continuance in time, duration. When we say "it is," we mean "it persists." Persistence is due to the power of being. Thus being is made possible by something the meaning of which extends beyond the concept of being. Being points beyond itself.

Accustomed as we are to think in terms of space, the expression "being points beyond itself" may be taken to denote a higher level in space. What is meant, however, is a higher category than being: the power of maintaining being.

Why does being continue to be? Any answer offered would add a concept indispensable to being, thus making it impossible to regard being as the one and only supreme concept.

Being is either open to, or dependent on, what is more than being, namely, the care for being, or it is a cul-de-sac, to be explained in terms of self-sufficiency. The weakness of the first possibility is in its reference to a mystery; the weakness of the second possibility is in its pretension to offer a rational explanation.

Nature, the sum of its laws, may be sufficient to explain in its own terms how facts behave within nature; it does not explain why they behave at all. Some tacit assumptions of the theory of insufficiency remain problematic.

How does one explain explanation? Is not self-sufficiency of nature a greater puzzle, transcending all explanations, than the idea of nature's being dependent on what surpasses nature? The idea of dependence is an explanation, whereas self-sufficiency is an unprecedented, nonanalogous concept in terms of what we know about life within nature. Is not self-sufficiency itself insufficient to explain self-sufficiency?

Being would cease to be if its duration were a matter of indifference to the power of being. Duration of being presupposes concern for being. Being is transcended by a concern for being.

Our perplexity will not be solved by relating human existence to a timeless, subpersonal abstraction which we call essence. We can do justice to human being only by relating it to the transcendent care for being.

The ultimate problem is not being, but concern for being. What precedes being is not nothingness, but rather concern for being; logos as well as *pathos*.

God is not reducible to being. He is God as One Who brings others into being, as One Who cares for other beings.

There is a care that hovers over being. Being is surpassed by concern for being. Being would cease to be were it not for God's care for Being.

What accounts for being? *Pathos,* a transcendent, transitive concern. The locus of moral values is in a setting defined by the presence of a transcendent concern. Life is tridimensional; every act can be evaluated by two coordinate axes, in which the abscissa is man, the ordinate is God.

The most important decision a thinker makes is reflected in what he comes to consider the most important problem. According to Albert Camus, "There is only one really serious philosophical problem: and that is suicide." May I differ and suggest that there is only one really serious problem: and that is martyrdom. Is there anything worth dying for?

We can only live the truth if we have the power to die for it. Suicide is escape from evil and surrender to absurdity. A martyr is a witness to the holy in spite of evil absurdity.

Nietzsche's formula for the greatness of a human being is *amor fati.* Jewish tradition would suggest as the formula for the greatness of man his capacity for *kiddush hashem,* readiness to die for the sake of God, for the sake of the Name.

And yet, even though God's creation retains precedence over man's corruption, man has the power to convert blessing into curse, to use being for undoing, to turn the elixir of God's word to deadly poison. His power of corruption may again and again, temporarily, for long stretches of history, destroy what God designs. However, man's willfulness is not the ultimate force in history. We are involved in a drama dependent upon the polarity of creation and corruption. Just as creation goes on all the time, redemption goes on all the time. At the end, we believe, God's care defeats man's defiance.

God and the world are not opposite poles. There is darkness in the world, but there is also this call, "Let there be light!" Nor are body and soul at loggerheads. We are not told to decide between "Either—Or," either God or the world, either this world or the world to come. We are told to accept Either and Or, God and the world. It is upon us to strive for a share in the world to come, as well as to let God have a share in this world.

Chapter six

How to live

Modern thinking has often lost its way by separating the problem of truth from the problem of living, cognition from man's total situation. Such separation has resulted in reason's isolationism, in utopian and irrelevant conceptions of man. Reflection alone will not procure self-understanding. The human situation is disclosed in the thick of living. The deed is the distillation of the self. We can display no initiative, no freedom in sheer being; our responsibility is in living.

Where does man come upon himself most directly? Is it in abstract self-consciousness, in the generality of "knowing that I am," of "knowing that I think"? Man encounters himself, he is surprised to know himself, in the words he utters, in the deeds he does, and above all in living as an answer.

It is living rather than sheer being that comes close to man's realness. Being may be applied to a dead horse, but it is the living man we are concerned with. Indeed, the categories used in describing both human being and being human are all the fruits of living.

As sheer being man dissolves in anonymity. But man is not only being, he is also living, and if he were simply to "surrender to being," as Heidegger calls upon us to do, he would abdicate his power to decide and reduce his living to being.

To be is both passive and intransitive. In living, man relates himself actively to the world. Deeds are the language of living, articulating the uniqueness of human being, the insights of being human.

The decisive form of human being is *human living*. Thus the proper theme for the study of man is the problem of living, of what to do with being. Living means putting being into shape, lending form to sheer being.

Human living is exceedingly common, exceedingly trite. The repetitiousness of doing, the stereotypes of speaking, deprive us of the dignity of living. Our ability to lend form to our being depends upon our understanding of the singularity of human living.

There is no guarantee or assurance of attaining significant being. It is a mistake to assume that significant being is achieved unwittingly, to let hours go on in order to arrive at the goals of living. Life is a battle for meaning which may be lost or won, totally or partially. What is at stake may be gambled away.

The root of creativity is discontent with mere being, with just being around in the world. Man is challenged not to surrender to mere being. Being is to be surpassed by living. The problem is how to live my being explicitly. Being human is living-in-the-world.

Insufficiency of mere being drives man to more-than-being, *to bring into being,* to come into meaning. We transcend being by bringing into being—thoughts, things, offspring, deeds.

If man's quest for supreme meaning is valid and required

by the truth of being human, and if that quest can only go on by relating oneself to transcendent meaning, then we must affirm the validity and requiredness of man's relating himself to transcendent meaning.

Man's plight, as said above, is not due to the fear of nonbeing, to the fear of death, but to the fear of living, because all living is branded with the unerasable shock at absurdity, cruelty, and callousness experienced in the past. A human being is a being in fear of pain, in fear of being put to shame.

Anguish is partly rooted in being human and partly due to misconceptions about one's own being as well as to social incompatibilities. The fear of living arises most commonly out of experiences of failure or insult, of having gone astray or having been rebuffed. It is rooted not in being but in the living of our being, in the encounter with other human beings, in not knowing how to be with other beings, in the inability or refusal to communicate, but above all in the failure to live in complete involvement with what transcends our living.

Our failure is due to our regarding the realm of values as a superstructure of existence, deriving the "ought" from the "is," "norms" from "facts," spirit from nature, requirement from measurement.

Human being shares the being of all beings, just as champagne and shoe polish, cheesecake and pebbles. Being human, however, cannot be classified or placed in the series of other beings. Being human, as said above, is an act not a thing. Its chief characteristic is not being but what is done with being.

Being human is the humanization of being, the transmutation of mute givenness. By being human man exceeds sheer being. Being is anonymous, silent. Humanization is articulation of meaning inherent in being.

In the ground of our being the awareness of participating in being does not offer any ultimate firmness. What drives us on mysteriously is the experience of being as an answer, an exclamation.

To be is to obey

Heidegger's rhetorical question, "Has the Dasein, as such, ever freely decided and will it ever be able to decide as to whether to come into existence or not?" has been answered long ago: "It is against your will that you are born, it is against your will that you live, and it is against your will that you are bound to give account. . . ." The transcendence of human being is disclosed here as life imposed upon, as imposition to give account, as imposition of freedom. The transcendence of being is commandment, being here and now is obedience.

I have not brought my being into being. Nor was I thrown into being. My being is obeying the saying "Let there be!"

Commandment and expectation lie dormant in the recesses of being and come to light in the consciousness of being human. What Adam hears first is a command.

Against the conception of the world as something just here, the Bible insists that the world is creation. Over all being stand the words: Let there be! And there was, and there is. To be is to obey the commandment of creation. God's word is at stake in being. There is a cosmic piety in sheer being. What is endures as a response to a command.

Philosophically the primacy of creation over being means that the "ought" precedes the "is." The order of things goes back to an "order" of God.

Even evading metaphysical reflection about the ultimate

97

source of being, an individual will confess that being does not come about as a result of a will to be, since this would presuppose the being of a will. My own existence is not the result of my will to exist. At one moment my life came about, and it is a mysterious loyalty within my substance that keeps me in being.

Man's will to be cannot be separated from his ought to be. Human being completely independent of norm is a figment of the imagination.

The loss of the sense of significant being is due to the loss of the commandment of being. Being is obedience, a response. "Thou art" precedes "I am." I am because I am called upon to be.

Being, as said above, is not the only dimension in which human existence finds itself. Characteristic of human existence is the mutual involvement of being and meaning.

What I suggest is not that first there is neutral being and then values. Being created implies being born in value, being endowed with meaning, receiving value. Living involves acceptance of meaning, obedience, and commitment.

Continuity

A person is responsible for what he is, not only for what he does. The primary problem is not how to endow particular deeds with meaning but rather how to live one's total being, how to shape one's total existence as a pattern of meaning.

Is there a possibility of facing human existence as a whole from infancy to old age, or is man capable of living only in fractions, of going through moments unrelated to one another?

The problem of living may be defined as a problem of reconciliation, of bringing about a *modus vivendi* for the self in relation to all that is, in the midst of which, and in relation to which, he exists; of coordinating the forces that operate in the domain of inner life.

Character education will remain ineffective if it is limited to the teaching of norms and principles. The concern must be not to instill timeless ideas but to cultivate the concrete person. Life is clay, and character is form. How to lend shape, to bring order into the complexity of my inner and outer life? How to coordinate impulses, drives, ambitions? How to simplify the self? The goal is to lend shape to existence, to endow all of life with form.

Right living is like a work of art, the product of a vision and of a wrestling with concrete situations.

We cannot, on the other hand, analyze man as a being only here and now. Not only here, because his situation is intentional with the situation of other men scattered far and wide all over the world. Not only now, because his total existence is, in a sense, a summation of past generations, a distillation of experiences and thoughts of his ancestors.

The authentic individual is neither an end nor a beginning but a link between ages, both memory and expectation. Every moment is a new beginning within a continuum of history. It is fallacious to segregate a moment and not to sense its involvement in both past and future. Humbly the past defers to the future, but it refuses to be discarded. Only he who is an heir is qualified to be a pioneer.

Self-abandonment, permissiveness, reduces existence to a process in which the power to create events is arrested. The wisdom of the individual is not sufficient for the appreciation of the ability to say "no" to oneself. If one fails to accept

99

the teaching of a tradition, one learns from cardinal experiences, from drastic failures or sudden outbursts of awareness, that self-denials are as important as self-satisfactions.

The teaching of our society is that more knowledge means more power, more civilization—more comfort. We should have insisted in the spirit of the prophetic vision that more knowledge should also mean more reverence, that more civilization should also mean less violence.

The failure of our culture is in demanding too little of the individual, in not realizing the correlation of rights and obligations, in not realizing that there are inalienable obligations as well as inalienable rights. Our civilization offers comfort in abundance and asks for very little in return. Ours is essentially a Yes education; there is little training in the art of saying "no" to oneself.

The most important ritual object is the altar, but the altars are being destroyed.

The precariousness of being human

Being human is a most precarious condition. It is not a substance but a presence, a whisper calling in the wilderness. Man is hard of inner hearing, but he has sharp, avid eyes. The power he unlocks surpasses the power that he is, dazzling him. He has a capacity for extravagance, sumptuousness, presumption. His power is explosive. Human being is boundless, but being human is respect for bounds. The human situation may be characterized as a polarity of human being and being human.

Being human is an imposition of human being on human nature. It requires resistance to temptation, strength in facing frustration, refusal to submit to immediate satisfactions. It can be discarded with ease and justify a confession: I am inhuman and everything human is alien to me.

There is a drive within us to resist the claim upon our conscience to cultivate existence in conformity with demands. The sense of indebtedness is first blunted and then swept away by pride and the love of property and power. All human and national relationships become reduced to one form only: some dominate, while others are dominated.

Man can be stiff-necked, callous, cruel, refusing to open himself, to hear, to see, to receive. Even the divine image can become converted into a satanic image.

Notwithstanding the inner tension between the claim to be human and the craving to be animal, the alternative is hardly realistic. Mankind has reached a point of no return to animality. Man turned beast becomes his opposite, a species *sui generis*. The opposite of the human is not the animal but the demonic.

Creation has not eliminated absurdity and nothingness. Darkness may be encountered everywhere, and the abyss of absurdity is always only one step away from us. There is always more than one path to go, and we are forced to be free—we are free against our will—and have the audacity to choose, rarely knowing how or why. Our failures glare like flashlights all the way, and what is right lies underground. We are in the minority in the total realm of being, and, with a genius for adjustment, we frequently seek to join the multitude. We are in the minority within our own nature, and in the agony and battle of passions we often choose to envy the beast. We behave as if the animal kingdom were our lost paradise, to which we are trying to return for moments of delight, believing that it is the animal state in which happiness consists. We have an endless craving to be like the beast, a nostalgic admiration for the animal within us. According to a contemporary scientist: "Man's greatest tragedy occurred when he ceased to walk on all fours and cut himself off from the animal world by assuming an erect position. If man had continued to walk horizontally, and rabbits had learned to walk vertically, many of the world's ills would not exist."

Man is continuous both with the rest of organic nature and with the infinite outpouring of the spirit of God. A minority in the realm of being, he stands somewhere between God and the beasts. Unable to live alone, he must commune with either of the two.

Both Adam and the beasts were blessed by the Lord, but man was also charged with conquering the earth and dominating the beast. Man is always faced with the choice of listening either to God or to the snake. It is always easier to envy the beast, to worship a totem and be dominated by it, than to hearken to the Voice.

Our existence seesaws between animality and divinity, between that which is more and that which is less than humanity: below is evanescence, futility, and above is the open door of the divine exchequer where we lay up the sterling coin of piety and spirit, the immortal remains of our dying lives. We are constantly in the mills of death, but we are also the contemporaries of God.

Man is "a little lower than the Divine" (Psalm 8:5) and a little higher than the beasts. Like a pendulum he swings to and fro under the combined action of gravity and momentum, of the gravitation of selfishness and the momentum of the divine, of a vision beheld by God in the darkness of flesh and blood. We fail to understand the meaning of our existence when we disregard our commitments to that vision. Yet only eyes vigilant and fortified against the glaring and superficial can still perceive God's vision in the soul's horror-stricken night of human folly, falsehood, hatred, and malice.

Because of his immense power, man is potentially the most wicked of beings. He often has a passion for cruel deeds that only fear of God can soothe, suffocating flushes of envy that only holiness can ventilate.

If man is not more than human, then he is less than human. Man is but a short, critical stage between the animal and the spiritual. His state is one of constant wavering, of soaring or descending. Undeviating humanity is nonexistent. The emancipated man is yet to emerge.

Man is more than what he is to himself. In his reason he may be limited, in his will he may be wicked, yet he stands in a relation to God which he may betray but not sever and which constitutes the essential meaning of his life. He is the knot in which heaven and earth are interlaced.*

Man's being a problem to himself is an expression of his being-challenged. The only exit from his plight is in realizing that his plight is a task rather than misery for misery's sake. We are both challenged and invited to answer what we face.

Being-challenged-in-the-world

An isolated self, "consciousness in general," human nature in the sense of self-sufficient, spontaneous behavior, uninfluenced by intellectual and social factors, is an abstraction.

The pathology of the self will not be understood unless the power that evokes being human, the ultimate evocation of

* See A. J. Heschel, *Man Is Not Alone*, pp. 210f.

the self, is properly understood. Boredom, for example, is a sickness of the self-consciousness, the result of one's inability to sense that vital evocation. Despair is due not to failures but to the inability to hear deeply and personally the challenge that confronts us.

How shall we account for this evocation in the heart of human being? Whence this concern for direction that transcends sheer being? It is, it seems, due to the fact that man in his very existence involves a commitment of which he is not conscious. This commitment is lodged neither in his memory nor in his subconscious, and yet it is operative and mysteriously present within existence.

To be sure, man has the power to suppress the challenge by stressing one drive above all others. This procedure often justified and hailed by an ideology amounts to the idolization of a particular drive. Yet, like all idolatry it is eventually abandoned. History is a vast panorama of idols worshiped and idols smashed.

The crisis of man is due to his failure to accept that challenge or, even when accepting it, to acknowledge it as the overriding problem of his total existence.

The world is a problem as well as a task. We find meaning by discovering that the problem is the task, in cultivating the art of sensing our part in the task, in the discovery that the world is a problem as well as an expectation.

Meaning insinuates itself into our existence. We cannot grab or conquer it, we can only be involved in it.

Human living is not simply being here and now, being around, a matter of fact; it is being in a dilemma, being cross-examined, called upon to answer. Man is not left alone.

Unlike the being of all other beings, man knows himself as

being exposed, challenged, judged, encountered. To be human is to be a problem. Is the wondering, wrestling, searching, and quandary a self-inflicted disease? Eliminate the challenge, the wrestling, and man will be deprived of his humanity. Being challenged is not man-made, an attitude, an awareness; it is an essential mode of his being.

The challenge comes upon me. The question is forced upon me. I seem unable to transcend my existence. Yet it is the question that transcends me, that upsets me. Whence does it come? Is it the structure of being human that has a built-in tendency to upset itself, to question itself?

To regard the awareness of being challenged as a myth is itself a myth. The human mind is capable of creating myths. But is the mind itself a myth?

Human living is being-challenged-in-the-world, not simply being-in-the-world. The world forces itself upon me, and there is no escape from it. Man is continuously exposed to it, challenged by it, to sense or to comprehend it. He cannot evade the world. It is as if the world were involved in man, had a stake in man.

The first thought a child becomes aware of is his being called, his being asked to respond or to act in a certain way. It is in acts of responding to demands made upon him that the child begins to find himself as part of both society and nature. Without the awareness of a task to be done, of a task waiting for him, man regards himself as an outcast. The content of the task we must acquire, the search for a task is given with consciousness.

The self is inescapably beset by the questions: What shall I do with my existence, with my being here and now? What does it mean to be alive? What does being alive imply for my will and intelligence? Its most characteristic condition is discontent with sheer being, generated by a challenge which is not to be derived from being around, being-here-too; it questions and transcends human being. Just as consciousness always posits an idea, as Brentano and Husserl have shown, self-consciousness posits a challenge. Consciousness of the self comes about in being challenged, in being called upon, in the choice between refusal and response.

Requiredness

Human living as being-challenged-in-the-world can be understood only in terms of requiredness, demand, and expectation. Significant living is an attempt to adjust to what is expected and required of a human being.

The sense of requiredness is as essential to being human as his capacity for reasoning. It is an error to equate the two as it is a distortion to derive the sense of requiredness from the capacity for reasoning.

The sense of requiredness is not an afterthought; it is given with being human; not added to it but rooted in it.

What is involved in authentic living is not only an intuition of meaning but a sensitivity to demand, not a purpose but an expectation. Sensitivity to demands is as inherent in being human as physiological functions are in human being.

A person is he of whom demands can be made, who has the capacity to respond to what is required, not only to satisfy his needs and desires. Only a human being is said to be responsible. Responsibility is not something man imputes to himself; he is a self by virtue of his capacity for responsibility, and he would cease to be a self if he were to be deprived of responsibility.

The qualities that constitute personhood, such as love, the passion for meaning, the capacity to praise, etc., can hardly be regarded as demands of reason, though reason must offer direction as to what is worthy of being loved or praised. Their justification is in their being required for being human.

Here is a basic difference between the Greek and the biblical conception of man. To the Greek mind, man is above all a rational being; rationality makes him compatible with the cosmos. To the biblical mind, man is above all a commanded being, a being of whom demands may be made. The central problem is not: What is being? but rather: What is required of me?

Greek philosophy began in a world without a supreme, living, one God. It could not accept the gods or the example of their conduct. Plato had to break with the gods and to ask: What is the good? And the problem of values was born. And it was the idea of values that took the place of God. Plato lets Socrates ask: What is good? Yet Moses' question was: What does God require of thee?

Indebtedness

The most significant intellectual act is to decide what the most fundamental question is to live by.

Ontology inquires: What is being? Epistemology inquires: What is thinking? The heart of man inquries: What is expected of me? Or in the language of the Bible: What is required of me?

The source of insight is an awareness of being called upon to answer. Over and above personal problems, there is an objective challenge to overcome inequity, injustice, helplessness, suffering, carelessness, oppression. Over and above the din of desires there is a calling, a demanding, a waiting, an expectation. There is a question that follows me wherever I turn. What is expected of me? What is demanded of me?

What we encounter is not only flowers and stars, mountains and walls. Over and above all things is a sublime expectation, a waiting for. With every child born a new expectation enters the world.

This is the most important experience in the life of every human being: something is asked of me. Every human being has had a moment in which he sensed a mysterious waiting for him. Meaning is found in responding to the demand, meaning is found in sensing the demand.

Indebtedness is given with our being human because our being is not simply being, our being is being created. Being created means, as said above, that the "ought" precedes the "is." The world is such that in its face one senses owingness rather than ownership. The world is such that in sensing its presence one must be responsive as well as responsible.

Indebtedness is given with our very being. It is not derived from conceptions; it lives in us as an awareness before it is conceptualized or clarified in content. It means having a task, being called. It experiences living as receiving, not only as taking. Its content is gratitude for a gift received. It is more than a biological give-and-take relationship.

Indebtedness is the pathos of being human, self-awareness of the self as committed; it is given with the awareness of existence. Man cannot think of himself as human without being conscious of his indebtedness. Thus it is not a mere feeling, but rather a constitutive feature of being human. To eradicate it would be to destroy what is human in man.

The sense of indebtedness, although present in the consciousness of all men, is translated in a variety of ways: duty, obligation, allegiance, conscience, sacrifice. Yet the content and direction of these terms are subject to interpretation.

There is no authenticity to human existence without a sense of indebtedness, without an awareness of a point where man must transcend the self, his interests, his needs, without the realization that existence involves both utilization and cele-bration, satisfaction and exaltation.

Knowing is not due to coming upon something, naming and explaining it. Knowing is due to something forcing itself upon us.

Thought is a response to being rather than an invention. The world does not lie prostrate, waiting to be given order and coherence by the generosity of the human mind. Things are evocative. When conceits are silent and all words stand still, the world speaks. We must burn the clichés to clear the air for hearing. Conceptual clichés are counterfeit; precon-ceived notions are misfits. Knowledge involves love, care for the things we seek to know, longing, being-drawn-to, being overwhelmed.

The experience of being asked

But to whom does man in his priceless and unbridled free-dom owe anything? Where does the asking come from? To whom is he accountable?

Religion has been defined as a feeling of absolute depen-dence. We come closer to an understanding of religion by defining one of its roots as a sense of personal indebtedness. God is not only a power we depend on, He is a God who demands. Religion begins with the certainty that something is asked of us, that there are ends which are in need of us.

Unlike all other values, moral and religious ends evoke in us a sense of obligation. Thus religious living consists in serving ends that are in need of us. Man is a divine need, God is in need of man. Religion is not a feeling for the mystery of living, or a sense of awe, wonder, or fear, which is the root of religion; but rather the question *what to do* with the feeling for the mystery of living, what to do with awe, wonder, or fear. Thinking about God begins when we do not know any more how to wonder, how to fear, how to be in awe. For wonder is not a state of aesthetic enjoyment. Endless wonder is endless tension, a situation in which we are shocked at the inadequacy of our awe, at the weakness of our shock, as well as the state of being asked the ultimate question.

The soul is endowed with a sense of indebtedness, and wonder, awe, and fear unlock that sense of indebtedness. Wonder is the state of our being asked.

In spite of our pride, in spite of our acquisitiveness, we are driven by an awareness that something is asked of us; that we are asked to wonder, to revere, to think, and to live in a way compatible with the grandeur and mystery of living.

What gives birth to religion is not intellectual curiosity but the fact and experience of our being asked.

All that is left to us is a choice—to answer or to refuse to answer. Yet the more deeply we listen, the more we become stripped of the arrogance and callousness which alone would enable us to refuse. We carry a load of marvel, wishing to exchange it for the simplicity of knowing what to live for, a load which we can never lay down or continue to carry not knowing where.

If awe is rare, if wonder is dead, and the sense of mystery defunct, then the problem of what to do with awe, wonder, and mystery does not exist, and one does not sense being asked. The awareness of being asked is easily repressed, for it is an echo of the intimation that is small and still. It will not, however, remain forever subdued. The day comes when the still small intimation becomes "like the wind and storm, fulfilling His word" (Psalm 148:8).

Indeed, the dead emptiness in the heart is unbearable to the living man. We cannot survive unless we know what is asked of us.

I am commanded—therefore I am

No one will question the reality and authenticity of the being of a stone. Yet how does man recognize and establish the reality of being human? Is not being human an arbitrary imposition? I never question my animality. But is humanity intrinsic to my being? Is not the very concept of humanity an illusion, a conceit, or an epiphenomenon? *De omnibus dubitandum.* Of one thing, however, I am sure. There is a challenge that I can never evade, in moments of failure as in moments of achievement. Man is inescapably, essentially challenged on all levels of his existence. It is in his being challenged that he discovers himself as a human being. Do I exist as a human being? My answer is: *I am commanded—therefore I am.* There is a built-in *sense of indebtedness in the consciousness of man,* an awareness of *owing gratitude,* of being *called upon* at certain moments to reciprocate, to answer, to live in a way which is compatible with the grandeur and mystery of living.

The ultimate validity of being human depends upon prophetic moments. If care, reciprocity, and the quest of man are self-induced or mere functions of the social organism, then being human must be regarded as an experiment—that failed. The reality of being human depends upon man's sense of indebtedness being a response to transcendent requiredness.

Without such awareness man is spiritually inane, neither creative nor responsible. Man is a commanded being, coming into meaning in sensing the demand.

Failure to understand what is demanded of us is the source of anxiety. The acceptance of our existential debt is the prerequisite of sanity.

The world was not made by man. The earth is the Lord's, not a derelict. What we own, we owe. "How shall I ever repay to the Lord all his bounties to me!" (Psalm 116:12).

Embarrassment

Let not the wise man glory in his wisdom, let not the mighty man glory in his might; but let him who glories glory in this: that he has a *sense of ultimate embarrassment*. How embarrassing for man to be the greatest miracle on earth and not to understand it! How embarrassing for man to live in the shadow of greatness and to ignore it, to be a contemporary of God and not to sense it. Religion depends upon what man does with his ultimate embarrassment. It is the awareness that the world is too great for him, the awareness of the grandeur and mystery of being, the awareness of being present at the unfolding of an inconceivable eternal saga.

Embarrassment is the awareness of an incongruity of character and challenge, of perceptivity and reality, of knowledge and understanding, of mystery and comprehension. Experiencing the evanescence of time, one realizes the absurdity of man's sense of sovereignty. In the face of the immense misery of the human species, one realizes the insufficiency of all human effort to relieve it. In the face of one's inner anguish, one realizes the fallacy of absolute expediency.

Embarrassment is a response to the discovery that in living we either replenish or frustrate a wondrous expectation. It involves an awareness of the grandeur of existence that may be wasted, of a waiting ignored, of unique moments missed. It is a protection against the outburst of the inner evils, against arrogance, *hybris,* self-deification. The end of embarrassment would be the end of humanity.

There is hardly a person who does not submit his soul to the beauty parlor, who does not employ the make-up of vanity in order to belie his embarrassment. It is only before God that we all stand naked.

Great is the challenge we face at every moment, sublime the occasion, every occasion. Here we are, contemporaries of God, some of His power at our disposal.

The honest man is humbled by the awareness that his highest qualities are but semiprecious; all ground for firmness is mud. Except for his will to cling to life, what is his abiding concern?

Embarrassment not only precedes religious commitment; it is the touchstone of religious existence. How embarrassing for man to have been created in the likeness of God and to be unable to recognize him! In the words of Job:

> Lo, He passes by me and I see Him not;
> He moves on, but I do not perceive Him.
> Job 9:11

The sense of embarrassment may be contrasted with the self-assurance of a nonreligious type: "I do not need a God to tell me how to live. I am a good person without going to the synagogue or church." A religious man could never say:

"I am a good person." Far from being satisfied with his conduct, he prays three times daily: "Forgive us, our Father, for we have sinned."

I am afraid of people who are never embarrassed at their own pettiness, prejudices, envy, and conceit, never embarrassed at the profanation of life. A world full of grandeur has been converted into a carnival. There are slums, disease, and starvation all over the world, and we are building more luxurious hotels in Las Vegas. Social dynamics is no substitute for moral responsibility.

I shudder at the thought of a society ruled by people who are absolutely certain of their wisdom, by people to whom everything in the world is crystal-clear, whose minds know no mystery, no uncertainty.

What the world needs is a sense of embarrassment. Modern man has the power and the wealth to overcome poverty and disease, but he has no wisdom to overcome suspicion. We are guilty of misunderstanding the meaning of existence; we are guilty of distorting our goals and misrepresenting our souls. We are better than our assertions, more intricate, more profound than our theories maintain. Our thinking is behind the times.

What is the truth of being human? The lack of pretension, the acknowledgment of opaqueness, shortsightedness, inadequacy. But truth also demands rising, striving, for the goal is both within and beyond us. The truth of being human is gratitude; its secret is appreciation.

Celebration

The power of being human is easily dissolved in the process of excessive trivialization. Banality and triteness, the by-products of repetitiveness, continue to strangle or corrode the sense of significant being. Submerged in everydayness, man begins to treat all hours alike. The days are drab, the nights revolt in the helplessness of despair. All moments are stillborn, all hours seem stale. There is neither wonder nor praise. What is left is disenchantment, the disintegration of being human.

How should one prevent the liquidation of one's power to experience everydayness as events? How should one ease the pressures of diluting human being to just being-around?

Events and the sense of surprise are not only inherent in the quintessence of reality and authentic consciousness, they are the points from which misunderstandings of human existence proceed. The question is not where is the event and what is the surprise, but how to see through the sham of routine, how to refute the falsehood of familiarity. Boredom is a spiritual disease, infectious and deadening, but curable.

The self is always in danger of being submerged in anonymity, of becoming a thing. To celebrate is to contemplate the singularity of the moment and to enhance the singularity of the self. What was shall not be again.

The biblical words about the genesis of heaven and earth are not words of information but words of appreciation. The story of creation is not a description of how the world came into being but a song about the glory of the world's having come into being. "And God saw that it was good" (Genesis 1:25). This is the challenge: to reconcile God's view with our experience.

We, however, live on borrowed notions, rely on past perceptions, thrive on inertia, delight in relaxation. Insight is a strain, we shun it frequently or even permanently. The demand, as understood in biblical religion, is to be alert and open to what is happening. What is, happens, comes about. Every moment is a new arrival, a new bestowal. How to welcome the moment? How to respond to the marvel?

The cardinal sin is in our failure not to sense the grandeur of the moment, the marvel and mystery of being, the possibility of quiet exaltation.

The secret of spiritual living is the power to praise. Praise is the harvest of love. Praise precedes faith. First we sing, then we believe. The fundamental issue is not faith but sensitivity and praise, being ready for faith.

To be overtaken with awe of God is not to entertain a feeling but to share in a spirit that permeates all being. "They all thank, they all praise, they all say: There is no one like God." As an act of personal recognition our praise would be fatuous; it is meaningful only as an act of joining in the endless song. We praise with the pebbles on the road which are like petrified amazement, with all the flowers and trees which look as if hypnotized in silent devotion.

To be human involves the ability to appreciate as well as the ability to give expression to appreciation. For thousands of years authentic existence included both manipulation and appreciation, utilization and celebration, both work and worship. In primitive society they were interdependent; in biblical religion they were interrelated. Today we face a different situation.

Man may forfeit his sense of the ineffable. To be alive is a commonplace; the sense of radical amazement is gone; the world is familiar, and familiarity does not breed exaltation or even appreciation. Deprived of the ability to praise, modern man is forced to look for entertainment; entertainment is becoming compulsory.

The man of our time is losing the power of celebration. Instead of celebrating, he seeks to be amused or entertained. Celebration is an active state, an act of expressing reverence or appreciation. To be entertained is a passive state—it is to receive pleasure afforded by an amusing act or a spectacle. Entertainment is a diversion, a distraction of the attention of the mind from the preoccupations of daily living. Celebration is a confrontation, giving attention to the transcendent meaning of one's actions.

Celebration is an act of expressing respect or reverence for that which one needs or honors. In modern usage, the term suggests demonstrations, often public demonstrations, of joy and festivity, such as singing, shouting, speechmaking, feasting, and the like. Yet what I mean is not outward ceremony and public demonstration, but rather inward appreciation, lending spiritual form to everyday acts. Its essence is to call attention to the sublime or solemn aspects of living, to rise above the confines of consumption.

To celebrate is to share in a greater joy, to participate in an eternal drama. In acts of consumption the intention is to please our own selves; in acts of celebration the intention is to extol God, the spirit, the source of blessing.

What is the purpose of knowledge? We are conditioned to believe that the purpose of knowledge is to utilize the world. We forget that the purpose of knowledge is also to celebrate God. God is both present and absent. To celebrate is to invoke His presence concealed in His absence.

The mind is in search of rational coherence, the soul in quest of celebration. Knowledge is celebration. Truth is more

117

than equation of thing and thought. Truth transcends and unites both thing and thought. Truth is transcendence, its comprehension is loyalty.

To the sense of indebtedness, the meaning of existence lies in reciprocity. In receiving a pleasure, we must return a prayer; in attaining a success, we radiate compassion. The world is not mere material for exploitation. We have the right to consume because we have the power to celebrate.

Since indebtedness is an essential ingredient of existence, the inability to celebrate is a sign of insolvency, of an inability to pay the existential debt.

There is no celebration without earnestness, without solemnity and reverence.

We are losing the power of appreciation; we are losing the ability to sing. Celebration without appreciation is an artificial, impersonal ceremony. A renewal of our strength will depend on our ability to reopen forgotten resources.

The meaning of existence is experienced in moments of exaltation. Man must strive for the summit in order to survive on the ground. His norms must be higher than his behavior, his ends must surpass his needs. The security of existence lies in the exaltation of existence.

This is one of the rewards of being human: quiet exaltation, capability for celebration. It is expressed in a phrase which Rabbi Akiba offered to his disciples:

A song every day,
A song every day.

Man in quest for an anchor in ultimate meaning is far from being a person shipwrecked who dreams of a palace while napping on the edge of an abyss. He is a person in full mastery of his ship who has lost his direction because he failed to remember his destination. Man in his anxiety is a *messenger who forgot the message.*

It is an accepted fact that the Bible has given the world a new concept of God. What is not realized is the fact that the Bible has given the world a new vision of man. The Bible is not a book about God; it is a book about man.

From the perspective of the Bible:

Who is man? *A being in travail with God's dreams and designs,* with God's dream of a world redeemed, of reconciliation of heaven and earth, of a mankind which is truly His image, reflecting His wisdom, justice, and compassion. God's dream is not to be alone, to have mankind as a partner in the drama of continuous creation. By whatever we do, by every act we carry out, we either advance or obstruct the drama of redemption; we either reduce or enhance the power of evil.